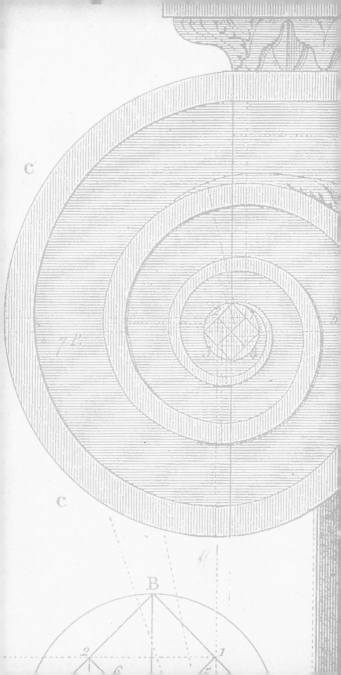

To:_____

In righteousness you will be established.

ISAIAH 54:14

From: _____

God's Words

of Life for

Dads

FROM THE

New International

Version

By

Robert Wolgemuth

inspirio

The gift group of Zondervan

GOD'S WORDS OF LIFE ON

ANGER

Better a patient man than a warrior,
a man who controls his temper than one
who takes a city.

PROVERBS 16:32

*Everyone should be quick to listen, slow to speak and
slow to become angry, for man's anger does not bring
about the righteous life that God desires.*

JAMES 1:19–20

*"In your anger do not sin": Do not let the sun go down
while you are still angry.*

EPHESIANS 4:26

Starting a quarrel is like breaching a dam;
so drop the matter before a dispute breaks out.

PROVERBS 17:14

A gentle answer turns away wrath,
but a harsh word stirs up anger.

PROVERBS 15:1

*Do not take revenge, my friends, but leave room for
God's wrath, for it is written: "It is mine to avenge; I
will repay," says the Lord.*

ROMANS 12:19

ANGER

Do not be quickly provoked in your spirit,
    for anger resides in the lap of fools.

ECCLESIASTES 7:9

A patient man has great understanding,
    but a quick-tempered man displays folly.

PROVERBS 14:29

A wise man fears the LORD and shuns evil,
    but a fool is hotheaded and reckless.
A quick-tempered man does foolish things,
    and a crafty man is hated.

PROVERBS 14:16-17

A hot-tempered man stirs up dissension,
    but a patient man calms a quarrel.

PROVERBS 15:18

Do not make friends with a hot-tempered man,
    do not associate with one easily angered,
or you may learn his ways
    and get yourself ensnared.

PROVERBS 22:24-25

*I want men everywhere to lift up holy hands in prayer,
without anger or disputing.*

1 TIMOTHY 2:8

ANGER

Love is patient, love is kind. It does not envy, it does not boast, it is not proud. It is not rude, it is not self-seeking, it is not easily angered, it keeps no record of wrongs.

1 CORINTHIANS 13:4-5

If your enemy is hungry, give him food to eat
if he is thirsty, give him water to drink.
In doing this, you will heap
burning coals on his head,
and the LORD will reward you.

PROVERBS 25:21-22

Anyone who is angry with his brother will be subject to judgment. ... Therefore, if you are offering your gift at the altar and there remember that your brother has something against you, leave your gift there in front of the altar. First go and be reconciled to your brother, then come and offer your gift.

MATTHEW 5:22-24

DEVOTIONAL THOUGHT ON ANGER

From the beginning of the account of Job and his trials, God collected Job's complaints like coupons. Then, in chapters 38 through 41, God visits the grocery store. Aisle by aisle, line by line, verse by verse, the Sovereign God gets ready to cash in his coupons at Job's checkout counter. Nowhere else in the Bible does God more thoroughly defend himself.

Taking a step back, the thing that I find the most striking about this monologue is neither God's outburst nor the fact of his right to defend himself. To me, the most amazing thing is that God chooses not to do this in other places in the Bible. Instead of putting people in their rightful place when they deserve it, God more often than not is merciful and slow to anger. So God's power is not revealed in his speech to Job. Rather it's revealed in his incredible restraint.

Every time you hold back from the lecture you think your family "deserves," you add more coupons. Now, take a lesson from God's actions in the Bible. Learn the power of mercy and restraint. Cash in these coupons only when the time comes to transform that withheld power into something truly important—and helpful—to your family.

COMMITMENT

Let us not become weary in doing good, for at the proper time we will reap a harvest if we do not give up.

GALATIANS 6:9

Be strong and do not give up, for your work will be rewarded.

2 CHRONICLES 15:7

Commit your way to the LORD;
    trust in him and he will do this:
He will make your righteousness
    shine like the dawn,
      the justice of your cause like the noonday sun.

PSALM 37:5-6

Love does not delight in evil but rejoices with the truth. It always protects, always trusts, always hopes, always perseveres.

1 CORINTHIANS 13:6-7

The LORD said, "I will give them singleness of heart and action, so that they will always fear me for their own good and the good of their children after them. I will make an everlasting covenant with them: I will

———

never stop doing good to them, and I will inspire them to fear me, so that they will never turn away from me."

JEREMIAH 32:39–40

Your hearts must be fully committed to the LORD our God, to live by his decrees and obey his commands.

1 KINGS 8:61

Place me like a seal over your heart,
 like a seal on your arm;
for love is as strong as death.

SONG OF SONGS 8:6

Anyone who runs ahead and does not continue in the teaching of Christ does not have God; whoever continues in the teaching has both the Father and the Son.

2 JOHN 9

LORD, who may dwell in your sanctuary?
 Who may live on your holy hill?
He whose walk is blameless
 and who does what is righteous,
who speaks the truth from his heart.

PSALM 15:1–2

COMMITMENT

Do not conform any longer to the pattern of this world, but be transformed by the renewing of your mind. Then you will be able to test and approve what God's will is—his good, pleasing and perfect will.

ROMANS 12:2

Jesus said, "I am coming soon. Hold on to what you have, so that no one will take your crown."

REVELATION 3:11

DEVOTIONAL THOUGHT ON
COMMITMENT

I knew Captain John K. Mitchell for two hours and fifty-five minutes, exactly the time it took to fly from Nashville to Phoenix. John was a naval officer, transferring to another plane in Phoenix. "Where's your wife?" I asked, having seen his wedding band.

"Oh, I lost Florence four years ago," he responded, his eyes telling me that the pain was still fresh. "During the time God gave us together, we lived by the verse, 'And we know that in all things God works for the good of those who love him.' God was so good to me to give me the years I did have with Florence."

John and Florence Mitchell had been married for sixty-six years. A full thirty years before her death, a stroke had mercilessly stricken her, rendering her an invalid. "I took care of her every single day," Captain Mitchell told me. "I wouldn't have had it any other way. It was my honor."

God may not work "all things" exactly according to our plans. But if we walk with our heavenly Father, if we obey his call, we will, like Captain John K. Mitchell, be able to look back and declare all things "good."

COMMUNICATION

May the words of my mouth
>   and the meditation of my heart
>   be pleasing in your sight, O LORD.

PSALM 19:14

From the fruit of his lips a man enjoys good things.

PROVERBS 13:2

The tongue of the righteous is choice silver.

PROVERBS 10:20

A wise man's heart guides his mouth,
>   and his lips promote instruction.

PROVERBS 16:23

*Speak to one another with psalms, hymns and spiritual
songs. Sing and make music in your heart to the Lord,
always giving thanks to God the Father for everything,
in the name of our Lord Jesus Christ.*

EPHESIANS 5:19–20

*Through Jesus ... let us continually offer to God a sac-
rifice of praise—the fruit of lips that confess his name.*

HEBREWS 13:15

COMMUNICATION

A word aptly spoken
>   is like apples of gold in settings of silver.

PROVERBS 25:11

Pleasant words are a honeycomb,
>   sweet to the soul and healing to the bones.

PROVERBS 16:24

A man finds joy in giving an apt reply—
>   and how good is a timely word!

PROVERBS 15:23

The Sovereign LORD has given me an
>   instructed tongue,
>   to know the word that sustains the weary.

ISAIAH 50:4

The tongue that brings healing is a tree of life.

PROVERBS 15:4

Always be prepared to give an answer to everyone who
asks you to give the reason for the hope that you have.
But do this with gentleness and respect, keeping a clear
conscience. . . .

1 PETER 3:15

COMMUNICATION

Speaking the truth in love, we will in all things grow up into him who is the Head, that is, Christ.

EPHESIANS 4:15

The tongue of the wise commends knowledge.

PROVERBS 15:2

Whoever of you loves life
    and desires to see many good days,
keep your tongue from evil
    and your lips from speaking lies.
Turn from evil and do good;
    seek peace and pursue it.

PSALM 34:12–14

An honest answer
    is like a kiss on the lips.

PROVERBS 24:26

Let your conversation be always full of grace, seasoned with salt, so that you may know how to answer everyone.

COLOSSIANS 4:6

If anyone speaks, he should do it as one speaking the very words of God.

1 PETER 4:11

DEVOTIONAL THOUGHT ON COMMUNICATION

When we were much younger, most of us heard the kids in the neighborhood chant, "Sticks and stones may break my bones, but words will never hurt me."

It's nonsense. Why? Because words are powerful. And, at times, they can hurt deeply.

Zerubbabel and his crew were busily rebuilding the temple that once had been the center of Jewish life. Enemies of the Jews from neighboring countries tried to hurt Zerubbabel and his associates—not with fists or weapons but with their words. They even sent in trained specialists ("counselors to work against them" [Ezra 4:1–5]) to extract the enthusiasm and joy from these faithful people. Zerubbabel defended their cause and countered the cruel and discouraging words that might have weakened his people's hands.

We also have the power of these "counselors"; our words can frighten our children and weaken the very ones we love. But, thankfully, we also can choose to imitate Zerubbabel in speaking good words that will encourage our kids. We can literally reverse fearfulness and give our families strength—just with the things we say.

Choose your words carefully. They have unbelievable power.

COURAGE

The LORD is my light and my salvation—
  whom shall I fear?
The LORD is the stronghold of my life—
  of whom shall I be afraid?

PSALM 27:1

"Do not fear, for I am with you;
  do not be dismayed, for I am your God,"
    declares the LORD.

ISAIAH 41:10

Be strong and courageous. Do not be terrified; do not be discouraged, for the LORD your God will be with you wherever you go.

JOSHUA 1:9

I can do everything through Christ who gives me strength.

PHILIPPIANS 4:13

Dear friends, do not be surprised at the painful trial you are suffering, as though something strange were happening to you. But rejoice that you participate in the sufferings of Christ, so that you may be overjoyed when his glory is revealed.

1 PETER 4:12-13

COURAGE

"When you pass through the waters,
    I will be with you;
and when you pass through the rivers,
    they will not sweep over you.
When you walk through the fire,
    you will not be burned;
    the flames will not set you ablaze,"
        declares the LORD.

ISAIAH 43:2

In all these things we are more than conquerors through him who loved us. For I am convinced that neither death nor life, neither angels nor demons, neither the present nor the future, nor any powers, neither height nor depth, nor anything else in all creation, will be able to separate us from the love of God that is in Christ Jesus our Lord.

ROMANS 8:37–39

Wait for the LORD;
    be strong and take heart
    and wait for the LORD.

PSALM 27:14

God gives strength to the weary
    and increases the power of the weak.

Even youths grow tired and weary,
    and young men stumble and fall;
but those who hope in the LORD
    will renew their strength.
They will soar on wings like eagles;
    they will run and not grow weary,
    they will walk and not be faint.

ISAIAH 40:29-31

*Do not be anxious about anything, but in everything,
by prayer and petition, with thanksgiving, present your
requests to God. And the peace of God, which transcends all understanding, will guard your hearts and
your minds in Christ Jesus.*

PHILIPPIANS 4:6-7

Strengthen the feeble hands,
    steady the knees that give way;
say to those with fearful hearts,
    "Be strong, do not fear;
your God will come,
    he will come with vengeance."

ISAIAH 35:3-4

DEVOTIONAL THOUGHT ON COURAGE

A small bookcase stood behind the overstuffed chair in the corner of my parents' living room. One of the volumes in that case was a huge book titled *Foxe's Book of Martyrs.* The tome was filled with actual accounts of individuals who, because of their love for Jesus Christ, were willing to die for him. I can vividly remember sitting on the floor behind that chair. Slowly I would turn the pages, my eyes fixed on the graphic drawings of how these incredibly courageous men and women gladly endured the most grisly torture imaginable instead of denying their loyalty and love for their Savior.

Although worldwide persecution of Christians continues today, it's safe to say that our defense of our Savior will probably never be as severe as these. But we are—and will be constantly—challenged to compromise what's right. Even today we may find ourselves looking at tempting circumstances and intimidating accusers. Although our loyalty to Jesus Christ may cost us, it will always be rewarding.

I love to envision Stephen and Jesus meeting in heaven. "Thank you," Jesus must have said to his loyal friend. "You're welcome," Stephen may have replied, "but you did it for me."

DECISIONS

"Counsel and sound judgment are mine;
I have understanding and power,"
Wisdom calls. ...
"I love those who love me,
and those who seek me find me."

PROVERBS 8:14, 17

The heart of the discerning acquires knowledge;
the ears of the wise seek it out.

PROVERBS 18:15

*If any of you lacks wisdom, he should ask God, who
gives generously to all without finding fault, and it will
be given to him. But when he asks, he must believe and
not doubt, because he who doubts is like a wave of the
sea, blown and tossed by the wind.*

JAMES 1:5–6

Help us, O God our Savior,
for the glory of your name.

PSALM 79:9

Trust in the LORD with all your heart
and lean not on your own understanding;
in all your ways acknowledge him,
and he will make your paths straight.

PROVERBS 3:5–6

DECISIONS

The LORD confides in those who fear him;
　　he makes his covenant known to them.

PSALM 25:14

It is God who works in you to will and to act according to his good purpose.

PHILIPPIANS 2:13

Make plans by seeking advice.

PROVERBS 20:18

Direct me in the path of your commands, O LORD,
　　for there I find delight.

PSALM 119:35

The Spirit of truth ... will guide you into all truth. He will not speak on his own; he will speak only what he hears, and he will tell you what is yet to come.

JOHN 16:13

The LORD will guide you always.

ISAIAH 58:11

"I guide you in the way of wisdom
　　and lead you along straight paths,"
　　　　says the LORD.

PROVERBS 4:11

DECISIONS

O LORD, direct my footsteps
    according to your word.

PSALM 119:133

Teach me to do your will, O LORD,
    for you are my God;
may your good Spirit
    lead me on level ground.

PSALM 143:10

Since you are my rock and my fortress, O LORD,
    for the sake of your name lead and guide me.

PSALM 31:3

In your unfailing love, O LORD, you will lead
    the people you have redeemed.

EXODUS 15:13

*Jesus said, "Do not let your hearts be troubled. Trust in
God; trust also in me."*

JOHN 14:1

Let him who walks in the dark,
    who has no light,
trust in the name of the LORD
    and rely on his God.

ISAIAH 50:10

DECISIONS

Show me the way I should go,
  for to you I lift up my soul, O LORD.

PSALM 143:8

In his heart a man plans his course,
  but the LORD determines his steps.

PROVERBS 16:9

"I will instruct you and teach you
  in the way you should go;
  I will counsel you and watch over you,"
    says the LORD.

PSALM 32:8

Listen to advice and accept instruction,
  and in the end you will be wise.

PROVERBS 19:20

*This is the confidence we have in approaching God:
that if we ask anything according to his will, he
hears us.*

1 JOHN 5:14

*You have known the holy Scriptures, which are able
to make you wise for salvation through faith in
Christ Jesus.*

2 TIMOTHY 3:15

DECISIONS

Solomon asked the Lord, "Give your servant a discerning heart to govern your people and to distinguish between right and wrong."

1 KINGS 3:9

Get wisdom, get understanding;
    do not forget my words or swerve from them.
Do not forsake wisdom, and she will protect you;
    love her, and she will watch over you.
Wisdom is supreme; therefore get wisdom.
    Though it cost all you have, get understanding.

PROVERBS 4:5-7

Your word, O LORD, is a lamp to my feet
    and a light for my path.

PSALM 119:105

The way of a fool seems right to him,
    but a wise man listens to advice.

PROVERBS 12:15

Show me your ways, O LORD,
teach me your paths;
    guide me in your truth and teach me,
for you are God my Savior,
    and my hope is in you all day long.

PSALM 25:4-5

Devotional Thought on Decisions

Being a good dad is a very tough job. Given a choice, every dad would prefer being liked by his family to not being liked. Unfortunately, there are many times in the lives of families when the dad would come in dead last on his kids' "Dad of the Year" nominee list. Leadership can be like that.

Poor Moses knew something about this. He had just been personally responsible for the release of over two million Jews from captivity, no small job. But now these people were being squeezed between the Red Sea and the entire Egyptian army. And they were very upset at Moses.

So Moses gives them a little talk: *Don't be afraid, hold steady, and watch God do this thing.* Given what looked like the ultimate rock-and-a-hard-place, how could he possibly have been so sure? The answer lies in the chapters leading up to this amazing story. Moses had kept in close contact with the Lord. His assurance came from God himself.

The secret to your success as a dad doesn't depend on how pleased your children are with your decisions. The key is in who is calling the shots for you.

DIFFICULT TIMES

Jesus said, "In this world you will have trouble. But take heart! I have overcome the world."

JOHN 16:33

God knows the way that I take;
    when he has tested me,
    I will come forth as gold.

JOB 23:10

Endure hardship ... like a good soldier of Christ Jesus.

2 TIMOTHY 2:3

It has been granted to you on behalf of Christ not only to believe on him, but also to suffer for him.

PHILIPPIANS 1:29

The Messiah was despised and rejected by men,
    a man of sorrows, and familiar with suffering.

ISAIAH 53:3

Just as the sufferings of Christ flow over into our lives, so also through Christ our comfort overflows.

2 CORINTHIANS 1:5

The LORD disciplines those he loves.

PROVERBS 3:12

DIFFICULT TIMES

Our present sufferings are not worth comparing with the glory that will be revealed in us.

ROMANS 8:18

If you are insulted because of the name of Christ, you are blessed, for the Spirit of glory and of God rests on you.

1 PETER 4:14

We ... rejoice in our sufferings, because we know that suffering produces perseverance; perseverance, character; and character, hope.

ROMANS 5:3–4

Consider it pure joy ... whenever you face trials of many kinds, because you know that the testing of your faith develops perseverance.

JAMES 1:2–3

The LORD has not despised or disdained
    the suffering of the afflicted one;
he has not hidden his face from him
    but has listened to his cry for help.

PSALM 22:24

DIFFICULT TIMES

———

For Christ's sake, I delight in weaknesses, in insults, in hardships, in persecutions, in difficulties. For when I am weak, then I am strong.

2 CORINTHIANS 12:10

A righteous man may have many troubles,
     but the LORD delivers him from them all.

PSALM 34:19

Blessed is the man who perseveres under trial, because when he has stood the test, he will receive the crown of life that God has promised to those who love him.

JAMES 1:12

Because he himself suffered when he was tempted, Jesus is able to help those who are being tempted.

HEBREWS 2:18

When I called, O LORD, you answered me;
     you made me bold and stouthearted.

PSALM 138:3

The Spirit helps us in our weakness. We do not know what we ought to pray for, but the Spirit himself intercedes for us with groans that words cannot express.

ROMANS 8:26

DIFFICULT TIMES

_____

Our struggle is not against flesh and blood, but against the rulers, against the authorities, against the powers of this dark world and against the spiritual forces of evil in the heavenly realms.

EPHESIANS 6:12

Fight the good fight of the faith. Take hold of the eternal life to which you were called.

1 TIMOTHY 6:12

Let the beloved of the LORD rest secure in him,
    for he shields him all day long,
and the one the LORD loves
    rests between his shoulders.

DEUTERONOMY 33:12

In the day of trouble
    the LORD will keep me safe in his dwelling;
he will hide me in the shelter of his tabernacle
    and set me high upon a rock.

PSALM 27:5

You have been my refuge, O God,
    a strong tower against the foe.
I long to dwell in your tent forever
    and take refuge in the shelter of your wings.

PSALM 61:3–4

DIFFICULT TIMES

———

He who dwells in the shelter of the Most High
    will rest in the shadow of the Almighty.

PSALM 91:1

O LORD, you have been a refuge for the poor,
    a refuge for the needy in his distress,
a shelter from the storm
    and a shade from the heat.

ISAIAH 25:4

We wait in hope for the LORD;
    he is our help and our shield.

PSALM 33:20

No discipline seems pleasant at the time, but painful.
Later on, however, it produces a harvest of righteousness
and peace for those who have been trained by it.

HEBREWS 12:11

Those who sow in tears
    will reap with songs of joy.
He who goes out weeping,
    carrying seed to sow,
    will return with songs of joy,
carrying sheaves with him.

PSALM 126:5-6

Devotional Thought on
Difficult Times

I read the story of the disciples challenging Jesus with a tough question about a blind man. "Who sinned, this man or his parents?" (John 9:2). When his disciples asked this question, Jesus answered, "This happened so that the work of God might be displayed in his life" (John 9:3).

You and I may live our lives with our eyesight intact. But we're going to experience pain, loss, doubt and grief. We will find ourselves questioning God's judgment in allowing us to be so severely set back. During those times, we need to remember that God's purposes are always the same. He acts, he moves, he decides our futures based on our circumstances' ability to deliver praise to his holy name.

Jesus healed the blind man. He may heal us or restore our net worth ... or not. But regardless, our task is—and will always be—to rest in his grace. Our charge is to take comfort that, though we may be in the midst of darkness, he is the light of the world.

Thank God for the pain. It provides for us the privilege of seeing ... and glorifying him.

ENCOURAGEMENT

Jesus said, "In this world you will have trouble. But take heart! I have overcome the world."

JOHN 16:33

God's mercy extends to those who fear him,
    from generation to generation.

LUKE 1:50

Cast all your anxiety on God because he cares for you.

1 PETER 5:7

In my alarm I said,
    "I am cut off from your sight!"
Yet you heard my cry for mercy, O LORD,
    when I called to you for help ...
Be strong and take heart,
    all you who hope in the LORD.

PSALM 31:22, 24

    My soul is downcast within me.
Yet this I call to mind
    and therefore I have hope:
Because of the LORD's great love
    we are not consumed,
        for his compassions never fail.
They are new every morning;

---

great is your faithfulness, O LORD.

LAMENTATIONS 3:20–23

Cast your cares on the LORD
and he will sustain you;
he will never let the righteous fall.

PSALM 55:22

Let the morning bring me word of
your unfailing love,
for I have put my trust in you, O LORD.

PSALM 143:8

The LORD is a refuge for the oppressed,
a stronghold in times of trouble.

PSALM 9:9

Why are you downcast, O my soul?
Why so disturbed within me?
Put your hope in God,
for I will yet praise him,
my Savior and my God.

PSALM 42:5

The eternal God is your refuge,
and underneath are the everlasting arms.

DEUTERONOMY 33:27

ENCOURAGEMENT

God is our refuge and strength,
an ever-present help in trouble.
Therefore we will not fear, though the earth give way
and the mountains fall into the heart of the sea,
though its waters roar and foam
and the mountains quake with their surging.

PSALM 46:1–3

I sought the LORD, and he answered me;
he delivered me from all my fears.

PSALM 34:4

My soul finds rest in God alone;
my salvation comes from him.
He alone is my rock and my salvation;
he is my fortress, I will never be shaken.

PSALM 62:1–2

When I said, "My foot is slipping,"
your love, O LORD, supported me.
When anxiety was great within me,
your consolation brought joy to my soul.

PSALM 94:18–19

The LORD upholds all those who fall
and lifts up all who are bowed down.

PSALM 145:14

ENCOURAGEMENT

I am the LORD, your God,
   who takes hold of your right hand
and says to you, Do not fear;
   I will help you.

ISAIAH 41:13

In all their distress the LORD too was distressed,
   and the angel of his presence saved them.
In his love and mercy he redeemed them;
   he lifted them up and carried them
   all the days of old.

ISAIAH 63:9

*Jesus said, "Come to me, all you who are weary and
burdened, and I will give you rest. Take my yoke upon
you and learn from me, for I am gentle and humble in
heart, and you will find rest for your souls."*

MATTHEW 11:28–29

*"I will refresh the weary and satisfy the faint," says
the LORD.*

JEREMIAH 31:25

*God says, "My grace is sufficient for you, for my power
is made perfect in weakness."*

2 CORINTHIANS 12:9

O LORD, you are my hiding place;
   you will protect me from trouble
   and surround me with songs of deliverance.

PSALM 32:7

Though I have fallen, I will rise.
Though I sit in darkness,
   the LORD will be my light.

MICAH 7:8

God, who has called you into fellowship with his Son
Jesus Christ our Lord, is faithful.

1 CORINTHIANS 1:9

The LORD is good to those whose hope is in him,
   to the one who seeks him.

LAMENTATIONS 3:25

Whatever is true, whatever is noble, whatever is right,
whatever is pure, whatever is lovely, whatever is
admirable—if anything is excellent or praiseworthy—
think about such things.

PHILIPPIANS 4:8

DEVOTIONAL THOUGHT ON ENCOURAGEMENT

If you were to drive past the football practice field just behind our local high school, you would see a wooden tower standing probably eighteen to twenty feet in the air. My guess is that very few people have any idea what it's for.

But you know, don't you? It's for the coaches during practice. Climbing up to the raised platform gives them a different look at various plays and strategies. It gives them perspective—something that can be a lot more difficult standing at ground level.

Joseph was despised by his brothers, sold like a dog, and thrown into prison on a bum rap. But God helped Joseph to "look down" on these events and realize that, in God's sovereign mercy, each had happened for his own good and for the survival of his family. Now there's a panoramic look.

What has happened to you and your family that makes you wonder if God knows what he's doing? Are you on the field, squashed by a three-hundred-and-fifty-pound linebacker and trying to figure out what's going on, or are you in the tower of God's perspective?

Ask him to lift you up. He's the very same God who lifted Joseph, and he'll do it for you.

FAILURE

We do not have a high priest who is unable to sympathize with our weaknesses, but we have one who has been tempted in every way, just as we are—yet was without sin. Let us then approach the throne of grace with confidence, so that we may receive mercy and find grace to help us in our time of need.

HEBREWS 4:15–16

The LORD God ... is with you. He will not fail you or forsake you.

1 CHRONICLES 28:20

Plans fail for lack of counsel,
> but with many advisers they succeed.

PROVERBS 15:22

If we are faithless,
> Christ will remain faithful,
> for he cannot disown himself.

2 TIMOTHY 2:13

The LORD is good,
> a refuge in times of trouble.
He cares for those who trust in him.

NAHUM 1:7

FAILURE

Though I walk in the midst of trouble,
    you preserve my life, O LORD;
you stretch out your hand
        against the anger of my foes,
        with your right hand you save me.

PSALM 138:7

We know that in all things God works for the good of
those who love him, who have been called according to
his purpose.

ROMANS 8:28

I lift up my eyes to the hills—
        where does my help come from?
My help comes from the LORD,
        the Maker of heaven and earth.

PSALM 121:1-2

Praise be to the God and Father of our Lord Jesus
Christ, the Father of compassion and the God of all
comfort, who comforts us in all our troubles, so that we
can comfort those in any trouble with the comfort we
ourselves have received from God.

2 CORINTHIANS 1:3-4

FAILURE

I said, "I have labored to no purpose;
>   I have spent my strength in vain and
>   for nothing.
Yet what is due me is in the LORD's hand,
>   and my reward is with my God."

ISAIAH 49:4

Stand firm. Let nothing move you. Always give your-
selves fully to the work of the Lord, because you know
that your labor in the Lord is not in vain.

1 CORINTHIANS 15:58

DEVOTIONAL THOUGHT ON
FAILURE

Many dads struggle with life. Sometimes things from their past can literally disable men. In some cases, these awful circumstances have become the reason why they have given up on life ... or have tragically failed.

Jesus was on his way to the temple feast when he passed a pool called Bethesda—the word means "a place of kindness." Tradition had it that when the water in this pool began to stir, the first person to touch it would be healed. There Jesus encountered a disabled man. As he did so often in working miracles of healing, Jesus changed this man's perspective, then he healed him ... heaping kindness upon kindness.

Have you been "disabled" by some past event in your life? Have you allowed this event to darken your past, hamper your present, and cast doubt on your future? If so, are you ready for Jesus' brand of kindness? Allow him to give you the will to heal your yesterday, and lavish you with wholeness for tomorrow.

FAITH

Faith is being sure of what we hope for and certain of what we do not see.

HEBREWS 11:1

Make every effort to add to your faith goodness; and to goodness, knowledge; and to knowledge, self-control; and to self-control, perseverance; and to perseverance, godliness; and to godliness, brotherly kindness; and to brotherly kindness, love.

2 PETER 1:5–7

Faith comes from hearing the message, and the message is heard through the word of Christ.

ROMANS 10:17

Abram believed the LORD, and he credited it to him as righteousness.

GENESIS 15:6

Let us fix our eyes on Jesus, the author and perfecter of our faith, who for the joy set before him endured the cross, scorning its shame, and sat down at the right hand of the throne of God.

HEBREWS 12:2

FAITH

———

"Have faith in God," Jesus answered. "I tell you the truth, if anyone says to this mountain, 'Go, throw yourself into the sea,' and does not doubt in his heart but believes that what he says will happen, it will be done for him. Therefore I tell you, whatever you ask for in prayer, believe that you have received it, and it will be yours."

MARK 11:22–24

In the gospel a righteousness from God is revealed, a righteousness that is by faith from first to last, just as it is written: "The righteous will live by faith."

ROMANS 1:17

We live by faith, not by sight.

2 CORINTHIANS 5:7

By faith Abraham, even though he was past age—and Sarah herself was barren—was enabled to become a father because he considered God faithful who had made the promise.

HEBREWS 11:11

Without faith it is impossible to please God.

HEBREWS 11:6

FAITH

[Trials] have come so that your faith—of greater worth than gold, which perishes even though refined by fire—may be proved genuine and may result in praise, glory and honor when Jesus Christ is revealed.

1 PETER 1:7

By faith we understand that the universe was formed at God's command, so that what is seen was not made out of what was visible.

HEBREWS 11:3

In his great mercy God has given us new birth into a living hope through the resurrection of Jesus Christ from the dead, and into an inheritance that can never perish, spoil or fade—kept in heaven for you, who through faith are shielded by God's power until the coming of the salvation that is ready to be revealed in the last time.

1 PETER 1:3-5

By faith Moses, when he had grown up, refused to be known as the son of Pharaoh's daughter. He chose to be mistreated along with the people of God rather than to enjoy the pleasures of sin for a short time. He regarded disgrace for the sake of Christ as of greater value than

———

the treasures of Egypt, because he was looking ahead to his reward.

HEBREWS 11:24-26

To all who received Christ, to those who believed in his name, he gave the right to become children of God—children born not of natural descent, nor of human decision or a husband's will, but born of God.

JOHN 1:12-13

Since we have been justified through faith, we have peace with God through our Lord Jesus Christ.

ROMANS 5:1

It is by grace you have been saved, through faith—and this not from yourselves, it is the gift of God—not by works, so that no one can boast.

EPHESIANS 2:8-9

Jesus said, "My Father's will is that everyone who looks to the Son and believes in him shall have eternal life, and I will raise him up at the last day."

JOHN 6:40

FAITH

God did not send his Son into the world to condemn the world, but to save the world through him. Whoever believes in him is not condemned. . . .

JOHN 3:17–18

Jesus said, "I tell you the truth, whoever hears my word and believes him who sent me has eternal life and will not be condemned; he has crossed over from death to life."

JOHN 5:24

Righteousness from God comes through faith in Jesus Christ to all who believe. There is no difference, for all have sinned and fall short of the glory of God, and are justified freely by his grace through the redemption that came by Christ Jesus.

ROMANS 3:22–24

It was not through law that Abraham and his offspring received the promise that he would be heir of the world, but through the righteousness that comes by faith. . . . The promise comes by faith, so that it may be by grace and may be guaranteed.

ROMANS 4:13, 16

Devotional Thought on Faith

Jairus grieved over his daughter's pain and pleaded with Jesus to heal her. Jesus was momentarily distracted after this request, and in the meantime several men came to Jairus with terrible news for him. This Daddy's girl was dead. Jairus was numb with grief.

Notice, however, Jesus' response in Mark 5:36. He didn't say anything about the dead girl. His first words were not a reassurance that the child was going to be all right. No, instead Jesus looked at this father and offered him the most incredible advice known to mankind: "Don't be afraid; just believe." Because you have read the whole story, you know that it has a happy—and absolutely miraculous—ending.

Jesus has some very sound advice for us hand-wringing fathers. He offers a bit of solace as we contemplate the need to care for and protect our children. "Don't be afraid; just believe."

Thank you, heavenly Father. I really needed that today.

FAITHFULNESS

The LORD rewards every man for his righteousness and faithfulness.

1 SAMUEL 26:23

Dear friend, you are faithful in what you are doing for the brothers, even though they are strangers to you.

3 JOHN 5

It is required that those who have been given a trust must prove faithful.

1 CORINTHIANS 4:2

[The administrators] could find no corruption in Daniel, because he was trustworthy and neither corrupt nor negligent.

DANIEL 6:4

The master replied, "Well done, good and faithful servant! You have been faithful with a few things; I will put you in charge of many things. Come and share your master's happiness!"

MATTHEW 25:21

A faithful man will be richly blessed. . . .

PROVERBS 28:20

FAITHFULNESS

I have kept the ways of the LORD;
    I have not done evil by turning from my God.
All his laws are before me;
    I have not turned away from his decrees.
I have been blameless before him
    and have kept myself from sin.
The LORD has rewarded me
    according to my righteousness,
    according to my cleanness in his sight.
To the faithful you show yourself faithful, O LORD,
    to the blameless you show yourself blameless.

2 SAMUEL 22:22–26

Righteousness and justice are the foundation
    of your throne;
    love and faithfulness go before you.
Blessed are those who have learned to acclaim you,
    who walk in the light
    of your presence, O LORD.

PSALM 89:14–15

May the LORD now show you kindness and faithfulness.

2 SAMUEL 2:6

Your love, O LORD, reaches to the heavens,
    your faithfulness to the skies.

PSALM 36:5

FAITHFULNESS

I will praise you with the harp
    for your faithfulness, O my God;
I will sing praise to you.

PSALM 71:22

Great is God's love toward us,
    and the faithfulness of the LORD
    endures forever.
Praise the LORD.

PSALM 117:2

O LORD, you are my God;
    I will exalt you and praise your name,
for in perfect faithfulness
    you have done marvelous things,
    things planned long ago.

ISAIAH 25:1

"I, the LORD, love justice. ...
In my faithfulness I will reward [my people]
    and make an everlasting covenant with them,"
      declares the LORD.

ISAIAH 61:8

*It gave me great joy to have some brothers come and
tell about your faithfulness to the truth and how you*

---

continue to walk in the truth.

3 JOHN 3

The LORD will cover you with his feathers,
and under his wings you will find refuge;
his faithfulness will be your shield and rampart.

PSALM 91:4

The works of God's hands are faithful and just;
all his precepts are trustworthy.
They are steadfast for ever and ever,
done in faithfulness and uprightness.

PSALM 111:7-8

I will bow down toward your holy temple
and will praise your name, O LORD,
for your love and your faithfulness,
for you have exalted above all things
your name and your word.

PSALM 138:2

The living, the living—they praise you, O LORD,
as I am doing today;
fathers tell their children
about your faithfulness.

ISAIAH 38:19

FAITHFULNESS

The fruit of the Spirit is love, joy, peace, patience, kind-
ness, goodness, faithfulness, gentleness and self-control.

GALATIANS 6:22–23

Let love and faithfulness never leave you
    bind them around your neck,
    write them on the tablet of your heart

PROVERBS 3:3

DEVOTIONAL THOUGHT ON FAITHFULNESS

Jesus called twelve men to follow him. Very little is said about what these men left behind, but ... here were a dozen men who must have wondered about their sanity ... leaving everything that was comfortable, familiar and safe to follow Jesus. With laser-beam clarity, the Master had taken aim at their wondering souls.

Choosing to be God's man in your home, in your town, or in your workplace may not earn you any immediate or visible commissions. You may experience rejection, alienation, and loneliness because of this decision. There will be times when you wonder if you've done the right thing. But Jesus' promise to you and me is certain: What we see today isn't all there is.

Someday, because of this partnership with our Savior, we will "rejoice ... and leap for joy." Many people have gone before us; they experienced this same uncertainty, and because they are with their heavenly Father today, their satisfaction is complete ... for all of eternity.

FATHERHOOD

We have all had human fathers who disciplined us and we respected them for it. How much more should we submit to the Father of our spirits and live! Our fathers disciplined us for a little while as they thought best; but God disciplines us for our good, that we may share in his holiness.

HEBREWS 12:9-10

When we were children, we were in slavery under the basic principles of the world. But when the time had fully come, God sent his Son, born of a woman, born under law, to redeem those under law, that we might receive the full rights of sons. Because you are sons, God sent the Spirit of his Son into our hearts, the Spirit who calls out, "Abba, Father." So you are no longer a slave, but a son; and since you are a son, God has made you also an heir.

GALATIANS 4:3-7

You know that we dealt with each of you as a father deals with his own children, encouraging, comforting and urging you to live lives worthy of God, who calls you into his kingdom and glory.

1 THESSALONIANS 2:11-12

FATHERHOOD

Fathers, do not exasperate your children; instead, bring them up in the training and instruction of the Lord.

EPHESIANS 6:4

Jesus said, "Which of you fathers, if your son asks for a fish, will give him a snake instead? Or if he asks for an egg, will give him a scorpion? If you then, though you are evil, know how to give good gifts to your children, how much more will your Father in heaven give the Holy Spirit to those who ask him!"

LUKE 11:11–13

Love the LORD your God with all your heart and with all your soul and with all your strength. These commandments that I give you today are to be upon your hearts. Impress them on your children. Talk about them when you sit at home and when you walk along the road, when you lie down and when you get up. Tie them as symbols on your hands and bind them on your foreheads. Write them on the doorframes of your houses and on your gates.

DEUTERONOMY 6:5–9

FATHERHOOD

I was young and now I am old,
     yet I have never seen the righteous forsaken
     or their children begging bread.
They are always generous and lend freely;
     their children will be blessed.

PSALM 37:25–26

I will open my mouth in parables,
     I will utter hidden things, things from of old—
what we have heard and known,
     what our fathers have told us.
We will not hide them from their children;
     we will tell the next generation
the praiseworthy deeds of the LORD,
     his power, and the wonders he has done.

PSALM 78:2–4

*As we have opportunity, let us do good to all people,
especially to those who belong to the family of believers.*

GALATIANS 6:10

DEVOTIONAL THOUGHT ON FATHERHOOD

The first chapter of Genesis contains the story of creation. Almighty God literally took nothingness and made something of it with the sound of his voice. He did what he did, he took a good look, and he was pleased. Interestingly enough, the rest of the Bible confirms that God kept looking, day after day. He paid attention.

Most dads will readily admit that they have a lot to learn. This is a whole new experience for us—something our formal education didn't include. So we learn as we go. We discover what works and what doesn't. But given God's example, we should rarely catch ourselves saying, "You know, I never saw it coming," "When did she start doing that?" or "I guess I just wasn't paying attention."

Our challenge is not just to live with our families but to really be there. To understand our job as the dad is to see what's going on—to not succumb to the temptation of getting on to the next thing without continuing to watch.

God's pattern was to create, to see, and to celebrate. That's a pretty good model to follow.

FEAR

The LORD is my light and my salvation—
 whom shall I fear?
The LORD is the stronghold of my life—
 of whom shall I be afraid?

PSALM 27:1

God will command his angels concerning you
 to guard you in all your ways;
they will lift you up in their hands,
 so that you will not strike your foot
 against a stone.
You will tread upon the lion and the cobra;
 you will trample the great lion and the serpent.
"Because he loves me," says the LORD,
 "I will rescue him;
 I will protect him, for he acknowledges
 my name."

PSALM 91:11–14

*You did not receive a spirit that makes you a slave
again to fear, but you received the Spirit of sonship.*

ROMANS 8:15

*God did not give us a spirit of timidity, but a spirit of
power.*

2 TIMOTHY 1:7

FEAR

"Do not be dismayed, for I am your God. I will strengthen you and help you; I will uphold you with my righteous right hand," says the LORD.

ISAIAH 41:10

Jesus said, "Do not be afraid, little flock, for your Father has been pleased to give you the kingdom."

LUKE 12:32

The Lord is my helper; I will not be afraid.

HEBREWS 13:6

When the servant of the man of God got up and went out early the next morning, an army with horses and chariots had surrounded the city. "Oh, my lord, what shall we do?" the servant asked. "Don't be afraid," the prophet answered. "Those who are with us are more than those who are with them." And Elisha prayed, "O LORD, open his eyes so he may see." Then the LORD opened the servant's eyes, and he looked and saw the hills full of horses and chariots of fire all around Elisha.

2 KINGS 6:15–17

There is no fear in love. But perfect love drives out fear. . . .

1 JOHN 4:18

FEAR

When you lie down, you will not be afraid;
>   when you lie down, your sleep will be sweet.
Have no fear of sudden disaster
>   or of the ruin that overtakes the wicked,
for the LORD will be your confidence
>   and will keep your foot from being snared.

PROVERBS 3:24–26

*Who shall separate us from the love of Christ? Shall
trouble or hardship or persecution or famine or naked-
ness or danger or sword? . . . No, in all these things we
are more than conquerors through him who loved us.*

ROMANS 8:35, 37

*Be strong and courageous. Do not be terrified; do not be
discouraged, for the LORD your God will be with you
wherever you go.*

JOSHUA 1:9

God is our refuge and strength,
>   an ever-present help in trouble.
Therefore we will not fear, though the earth give way
>   and the mountains fall into the heart of the sea.

PSALM 46:1–2

FEAR

My flesh and my heart may fail,
>   but God is the strength of my heart
>   and my portion forever.

PSALM 73:26

*Stand firm and you will see the deliverance the LORD
will bring you today.*

EXODUS 14:13

In righteousness you will be established:
Tyranny will be far from you;
>   you will have nothing to fear.
Terror will be far removed;
>   it will not come near you.

ISAIAH 54:14

Though an army besiege me,
>   my heart will not fear;
though war break out against me,
>   even then will I be confident.

PSALM 27:3

Even though I walk
>   through the valley of the shadow of death,
I will fear no evil.

PSALM 23:4

FEAR

If God is for us, who can be against us?

ROMANS 8:31

The LORD is with me; I will not be afraid.

PSALM 118:6

When I am afraid,
I will trust in you, O God.

PSALM 56:3

We were harassed at every turn—conflicts on the outside, fears within. But God, who comforts the downcast, comforted us.

2 CORINTHIANS 7:5-6

Devotional Thought on Fear

Daniel was courageous because he had been obedient to God all along—both in the small things and in the big things. If he hadn't trained himself to obey God every day by always telling the truth, doing his job well, and treating others with kindness, he probably would have buckled when he heard the king's decree not to worship anyone but him. He probably would have thought, "God will understand if I don't pray to him just this time. It's only for thirty days."

But Daniel refused to dishonor God. After all, he had seen God rescue Shadrach, Meshach, and Abednego from the fiery furnace. Daniel knew that God cared about him, and he knew that God takes care of his children. So he faced what could have been his death with courage. And how did God repay him? He sent an angel to close those lions' mouths.

The same God who protected Daniel from the lions is working in our lives today. So when trouble strikes, do what Daniel did—"he got down on his knees and prayed, giving thanks to his God, just as he had done before" (Daniel 6:10).

FORGIVENESS

Blessed are they
    whose transgressions are forgiven,
    whose sins are covered.
Blessed is the man
    whose sin the Lord will never
    count against him.

ROMANS 4:7-8

When you stand praying, if you hold anything against anyone, forgive him, so that your Father in heaven may forgive you your sins.

MARK 11:25

As far as the east is from the west,
    so far has God removed our
    transgressions from us.

PSALM 103:12

When you were dead in your sins . . . , God made you alive with Christ. He forgave us all our sins, having canceled the written code, with its regulations, that was against us and that stood opposed to us; he took it away, nailing it to the cross.

COLOSSIANS 2:13-14

FORGIVENESS

Bear with each other and forgive whatever grievances you may have against one another. Forgive as the Lord forgave you.

COLOSSIANS 3:13

"Come now, let us reason together,"
    says the LORD,
"Though your sins are like scarlet,
    they shall be as white as snow;
though they are red as crimson,
    they shall be like wool.

ISAIAH 1:18

In Christ we have redemption through his blood, the forgiveness of sins, in accordance with the riches of God's grace that he lavished on us with all wisdom and understanding.

EPHESIANS 1:7-8

God has rescued us from the dominion of darkness and brought us into the kingdom of the Son he loves.

COLOSSIANS 1:13

You are forgiving and good, O Lord,
    abounding in love to all who call to you.

PSALM 86:5

FORGIVENESS

The Lord our God is merciful and forgiving, even though we have rebelled against him.

DANIEL 9:9

Who is a God like you,
    who pardons sin and forgives the transgression
    of the remnant of his inheritance?
You do not stay angry forever
    but delight to show mercy.

MICAH 7:18

Repent and be baptized, every one of you, in the name of Jesus Christ for the forgiveness of your sins. And you will receive the gift of the Holy Spirit. The promise is for you and your children and for all who are far off—for all whom the Lord our God will call.

ACTS 2:38-39

The LORD is slow to anger, abounding in love and forgiving sin and rebellion.

NUMBERS 14:18

Forgive all our sins, O LORD,
and receive us graciously
    that we may offer the fruit of our lips.

HOSEA 14:2

FORGIVENESS

Father, forgive us our debts,
  as we also have forgiven our debtors.
And lead us not into temptation,
but deliver us from the evil one.

MATTHEW 6:12-13

Praise be to the Lord, the God of Israel,
    because he has come
    and has redeemed his people.

LUKE 1:68

*When the time had fully come, God sent his Son, born
of a woman, born under law, to redeem those under
law, that we might receive the full rights of sons.*

GALATIANS 4:4-5

He who conceals his sins does not prosper,
    but whoever confesses and renounces them
    finds mercy.

PROVERBS 28:13

Return to the LORD your God,
    for he is gracious and compassionate,
slow to anger and abounding in love,
    and he relents from sending calamity.

JOEL 2:13

FORGIVENESS

When we were overwhelmed by sins,
   you forgave our transgressions, O LORD.

PSALM 65:3

*If you forgive men when they sin against you, your
heavenly Father will also forgive you.*

MATTHEW 6:14

In Christ God forgave you.

EPHESIANS 4:32

*Jesus said, "If your brother sins, rebuke him, and if he
repents, forgive him. If he sins against you seven times
in a day, and seven times comes back to you and says, 'I
repent,' forgive him."*

LUKE 17:3-4

*The Lord said, "If my people, who are called by my
name, will humble themselves and pray and seek my
face and turn from their wicked ways, then will I hear
from heaven and will forgive their sin and will heal
their land."*

2 CHRONICLES 7:14

FORGIVENESS

Wash away all my iniquity
and cleanse me from my sin, O LORD.

PSALM 51:2

*You are a forgiving God, gracious and compassionate,
slow to anger and abounding in love.*

NEHEMIAH 9:17

*God was pleased to have all his fullness dwell in Christ,
and through him to reconcile to himself all things,
whether things on earth or things in heaven, by making
peace through his blood, shed on the cross.*

COLOSSIANS 1:19–20

Your sins have been forgiven on account of Jesus' name.

1 JOHN 2:12

*Let us not love with words or tongue but with actions
and in truth. This then is how we know that we belong
to the truth, and how we set our hearts at rest in God's
presence whenever our hearts condemn us. For God is
greater than our hearts, and he knows everything.*

1 JOHN 3:18–20

FORGIVENESS

Jesus said, "Two men owed money to a certain money-lender. One owed him five hundred denarii, and the other fifty. Neither of them had the money to pay him back, so he canceled the debts of both. Now which of them will love him more?"

Simon replied, "I suppose the one who had the bigger debt canceled."

"You have judged correctly," Jesus answered.

LUKE 7:41–43

If we confess our sins, God is faithful and just and will forgive us our sins and purify us from all unrighteousness.

I JOHN 1:9

DEVOTIONAL THOUGHT ON FORGIVENESS

The word "hate" was rarely used around our house. Very early in their lives, our daughters learned that, unless they were talking about monsters or poisonous snakes, they couldn't use this word.

However, notwithstanding this house rule that I personally enforced, there was an object I grew up hating as much as monsters and poisonous snakes. The object was a black-and-gray-speckled spiral-bound, eight-by-ten book, and each of my teachers had one on their desks. Printed on the cover were the words "Student Records."

Why did I feel so strongly? Because these record books contained inside information about me. They recorded every late paper, every failing grade, every citizenship faux pas ... everything I didn't want anyone to know.

King David lived a life filled with tardiness, failure, and poor citizenship. And he knew what it was to have all of these marks indelibly inscribed on the public record.

Because of his willingness to confess his sin, is it any wonder that David wrote the opening lines to Psalm 32? Can you blame him for referring to the forgiven person as "blessed"? It's as though the despised record book found its way to the desk's precipice, fell into the trash can and was delivered to the city dump for burning.

Confess your sins. Watch them burn. Then bask in the love and embrace of your Teacher and Savior.

FRIENDSHIP

A man of many companions may come to ruin,
    but there is a friend who sticks closer
    than a brother.

PROVERBS 18:24

Two are better than one,
    because they have a good return for their work:
If one falls down,
    his friend can help him up.
But pity the man who falls
    and has no one to help him up!
Also, if two lie down together, they will keep warm.
    But how can one keep warm alone?
Though one may be overpowered,
    two can defend themselves.
A cord of three strands is not quickly broken.

ECCLESIASTES 4:9–12

Wounds from a friend can be trusted.

PROVERBS 27:6

Perfume and incense bring joy to the heart,
    and the pleasantness of one's friend
    springs from his earnest counsel.

PROVERBS 27:9

FRIENDSHIP

Be devoted to one another in brotherly love. Honor one another above yourselves.

ROMANS 12:10

If we walk in the light, as God is in the light, we have fellowship with one another.

1 JOHN 1:7

Jesus said, "Greater love has no one than this, that he lay down his life for his friends. You are my friends if you do what I command. I no longer call you servants, because a servant does not know his master's business. Instead, I have called you friends."

JOHN 15:13–15

A friend loves at all times,
 and a brother is born for adversity.

PROVERBS 17:17

My intercessor is my friend
 as my eyes pour out tears to God.

JOB 16:20

FRIENDSHIP

He who loves a pure heart
and whose speech is gracious
will have the king for his friend.

PROVERBS 22:11

*Ruth told Naomi, "Where you go I will go, and where
you stay I will stay. Your people will be my people and
your God my God. Where you die I will die, and there
I will be buried. May the LORD deal with me, be it
ever so severely, if anything but death separates you
and me."*

RUTH 1:16–17

DEVOTIONAL THOUGHT ON
FRIENDSHIP

Jesus tells us to love everyone, even our enemies (Luke 6:27, 35). But Proverbs 13:20 says that if we are to grow wise, we must walk with wise people. If we choose "fools" as companions, we'll suffer harm.

A "companion" is much more than an acquaintance; he or she is one who becomes a close friend, a "traveling buddy," even a mate. If we choose companions who don't love God or don't act according to his Word, we're told in no uncertain terms that we're walking straight into trouble.

As dads, our job is to protect our children from harm. Therefore our job is to teach them to choose friends wisely. And this lesson is every bit as important for us as it is for our kids. Our companions are either making us wiser or leading us right into harm's way.

The Bible doesn't contradict itself at all on this issue. Love your neighbor. Love your enemy. But choose your friends with care.

GIVING

*God who supplies seed to the sower and bread for food
will also supply and increase your store of seed and will
enlarge the harvest of your righteousness. You will be
made rich in every way so that you can be generous on
every occasion, and through us your generosity will
result in thanksgiving to God. This service that you per-
form is not only supplying the needs of God's people but
is also overflowing in many expressions of thanks to
God. Because of the service by which you have proved
yourselves, men will praise God for the obedience that
accompanies your confession of the gospel of Christ, and
for your generosity in sharing with them and with
everyone else.*

2 CORINTHIANS 9:10-13

*Jesus sat down opposite the place where the offerings
were put and watched the crowd putting their money
into the temple treasury. Many rich people threw in
large amounts. But a poor widow came and put in two
very small copper coins, worth only a fraction of a
penny. Calling his disciples to him, Jesus said, "I tell
you the truth, this poor widow has put more into the
treasury than all the others. They all gave out of their
wealth; but she, out of her poverty, put in everything—
all she had to live on."*

MARK 12:41-44

GIVING

"Bring the whole tithe into the storehouse, that there may be food in my house. Test me in this," says the LORD Almighty, "and see if I will not throw open the floodgates of heaven and pour out so much blessing that you will not have room enough for it."

MALACHI 3:10

If they obey and serve God,
> they will spend the rest of their days in
> prosperity and their years in contentment.

JOB 36:11

Give, and it will be given to you. A good measure, pressed down, shaken together and running over, will be poured into your lap. For with the measure you use, it will be measured to you.

LUKE 6:38

Be openhanded and freely lend [your poor brother] whatever he needs ... Give generously to him and do so without a grudging heart; then because of this the LORD your God will bless you in all your work and in everything you put your hand to.

DEUTERONOMY 15:8, 10

GIVING

Store up for yourselves treasures in heaven, where moth and rust do not destroy, and where thieves do not break in and steal. For where your treasure is, there your heart will be also.

MATTHEW 6:20–21

"It is more blessed to give than to receive."

ACTS 20:35

Do not forget to do good and to share with others, for with such sacrifices God is pleased.

HEBREWS 13:16

Whoever sows sparingly will also reap sparingly, and whoever sows generously will also reap generously. Each man should give what he has decided in his heart to give, not reluctantly or under compulsion, for God loves a cheerful giver. And God is able to make all grace abound to you, so that in all things at all times, having all that you need, you will abound in every good work.

2 CORINTHIANS 9:6–8

God is not unjust; he will not forget your work and the love you have shown him as you have helped his people and continue to help them.

HEBREWS 6:10

Giving

Jesus said, "If anyone gives even a cup of cold water to one of these little ones because he is my disciple, I tell you the truth, he will certainly not lose his reward."

MATTHEW 10:42

A generous man will himself be blessed,
    for he shares his food with the poor.

PROVERBS 22:9

He who refreshes others will himself be refreshed.

PROVERBS 11:25

He who is kind to the poor lends to the LORD,
    and he will reward him for what he has done.

PROVERBS 19:17

If you spend yourselves in behalf of the hungry
    and satisfy the needs of the oppressed,
then your light will rise in the darkness,
    and your night will become like the noonday.
The LORD will guide you always;
    he will satisfy your needs in a sun-scorched land
    and will strengthen your frame.
You will be like a well-watered garden,
    like a spring whose waters never fail.

ISAIAH 58:10-11

GIVING

———

Jesus will say, "I was hungry and you gave me something to eat, I was thirsty and you gave me something to drink, I was a stranger and you invited me in, I needed clothes and you clothed me, I was sick and you looked after me, I was in prison and you came to visit me." Then the righteous will answer him, "Lord, when did we see you hungry and feed you, or thirsty and give you something to drink? When did we see you a stranger and invite you in, or needing clothes and clothe you? When did we see you sick or in prison and go to visit you?" Jesus will reply, "I tell you the truth, whatever you did for one of the least of these brothers of mine, you did for me."

MATTHEW 25:35–40

Honor the LORD with your wealth,
　　with the firstfruits of all your crops;
then your barns will be filled to overflowing,
　　and your vats will brim over with new wine.

PROVERBS 3:9–10

Peter said, "Silver or gold I do not have, but what I have I give you."

ACTS 3:6

DEVOTIONAL THOUGHT ON GIVING

As incredible as this sounds, my grandfather never locked the doors of his home. "If someone comes to our house in need, they're welcome to anything we have here," he told me. As a child, I never saw my dad handle an offering plate without putting something into it—even on vacation. No doubt he also wanted his children to witness the satisfaction of giving.

Because I had seen this modeled and truly didn't know any other way to act, our girls will tell you that, thanks to his dad and his grandfather, their dad does the same thing. There is joy in the simple act of giving. Stewardship is its own reward. Another way of saying this might be that a man is measured not by how much he has but by how much he gives away.

The members of the early church knew about this. They "shared everything they had. ... There were no needy persons among them" (Acts 4:32, 34). Those who had been blessed with possessions turned their attention away from their own success and lavished their good fortune on others.

Dads can be the best teachers on the subject of giving. How generous will your children be?

GOD'S CARE

Jesus said, "I am the good shepherd. The good shepherd lays down his life for the sheep."

JOHN 10:11

The righteous cry out, and the LORD hears them;
    he delivers them from all their troubles.
The LORD is close to the brokenhearted
    and saves those who are crushed in spirit.

PSALM 34:17–18

Look at the birds of the air; they do not sow or reap or store away in barns, and yet your heavenly Father feeds them. Are you not much more valuable than they?

MATTHEW 6:26

Jesus said, "Do not be afraid, little flock, for your Father has been pleased to give you the kingdom."

LUKE 12:32

LORD, you establish peace for us;
    all that we have accomplished
    you have done for us.

ISAIAH 26:12

Jesus said, "My sheep listen to my voice; I know them, and they follow me. I give them eternal life, and they

———

shall never perish; no one can snatch them out of my hand. My Father, who has given them to me, is greater than all; no one can snatch them out of my Father's hand."

JOHN 10:27-29

Praise the LORD, O my soul,
 and forget not all his benefits—
who forgives all your sins
 and heals all your diseases,
who redeems your life from the pit
 and crowns you with love and compassion,
who satisfies your desires with good things
 so that your youth is renewed like the eagle's.

PSALM 103:2-5

The eyes of all look to you, O LORD,
 and you give them their food
 at the proper time.
You open your hand
 and satisfy the desires of every living thing.

PSALM 145:15-16

Praise be to the Lord, to God our Savior,
 who daily bears our burdens.

PSALM 68:19

You, O LORD, have helped me and comforted me.

PSALM 86:17

The LORD will keep you from all harm—
    he will watch over your life;
the LORD will watch over your coming and
    going both now and forevermore.

PSALM 121:7-8

*Jesus said, "Surely I am with you always, to the very
end of the age."*

MATTHEW 28:20

The LORD your God is with you,
    he is mighty to save.
He will take great delight in you,
    he will quiet you with his love,
    he will rejoice over you with singing.

ZEPHANIAH 3:17

The LORD tends his flock like a shepherd:
    He gathers the lambs in his arms
and carries them close to his heart;
    he gently leads those that have young.

ISAIAH 40:11

DEVOTIONAL THOUGHT ON
GOD'S CARE

One summer we were castle-hopping in Europe. These structures were unbelievable. As I was standing in the courtyard of one particular palace and studying the intricate stonework, something dawned on me. These structures weren't just fancy homes; they were fortresses, built to protect a king or nobleman's family and a few hundred of his closest friends during hostile times. The thick walls, towering turrets, and draw-bridges were more than mere decoration.

You and I live in a war zone. The internal and external forces that seek to take us and our families hostage are as real today as the warriors who once tried to besiege those European castles. But God has built up our homes to be like fortresses; he protects them with his own foot soldiers.

When we overlook the fact that we are living in a war zone, our appreciation for God's loving protection diminishes in value. But when we truly pay attention to this fact, then our hearts should be filled with gratitude for his wings, his eyes, his hands, and his tireless angels standing guard.

Hope

This God is our God for ever and ever;
    he will be our guide even to the end.

PSALM 48:14

O LORD, you discern my going out
    and my lying down;
    you are familiar with all my ways.

PSALM 139:3

You are God my Savior,
    and my hope is in you all day long.

PSALM 25:5

Put your hope in the LORD,
    for with the LORD is unfailing love
    and with him is full redemption.

PSALM 130:7

*We have put our hope in the living God, who is the
Savior of all men, and especially of those who believe.*

1 TIMOTHY 4:10

Put your hope in the LORD
    both now and forevermore.

PSALM 131:3

HOPE

If you devote your heart to God
and stretch our your hands to him, ...
You will be secure, because there is hope;
you will look about you and take your
rest in safety.

JOB 11:13, 18

Find rest, O my soul, in God alone;
my hope comes from him.

PSALM 62:5

Wisdom is sweet to your soul;
if you find it, there is a future hope for you,
and your hope will not be cut off.

PROVERBS 24:14

"You will know that I am the LORD;
those who hope in me
will not be disappointed," says the LORD.

ISAIAH 49:23

*Against all hope, Abraham in hope believed and so
became the father of many nations.*

ROMANS 4:18

HOPE

———

Hope does not disappoint us, because God has poured out his love into our hearts by the Holy Spirit, whom he has given us.

ROMANS 5:5

You believe in God, who raised Christ from the dead and glorified him, and so your faith and hope are in God.

1 PETER 1:21

DEVOTIONAL THOUGHT ON HOPE

Only twice in my life have I tried my hand at organized football, but in my limited experience, I have had the experience of knowing what "the pile" feels like. This happens when the ball carrier is tackled and those closest to him, whether teammates or opponents, pile themselves up like cordwood on this hapless player. One consistent football rule from junior high to the big-time is: When the play is over, no additional players can join the pile. In other words, no piling on.

As you read the book of Job, you realize that every single person who knew Job had piled on top of him. At times he even thought he felt God's heft on the pile. But verse 19:25, "I know that my Redeemer lives," was written in the crush of this setting.

Some days we can truly identify with Job under the pile. The Scripture's encouragement is a simple one, though. Regardless of the weight, the pain, the frustration, the inability to breath under the pressure, our God is still standing. Take a deep breath. Look up from the mash and be glad. Your Redeemer has come.

IDENTITY

God said, "Let us make man in our image, in our like-ness, and let them rule over the fish of the sea and the birds of the air, over the livestock, over all the earth, and over all the creatures that move along the ground." So God created man in his own image, in the image of God he created him; male and female he created them.

GENESIS 1:26–27

O LORD, you created my inmost being;
    you knit me together in my mother's womb.
I praise you because I am
    fearfully and wonderfully made;
    your works are wonderful,
    I know that full well.

PSALM 139:13–14

"Before I formed you in the womb I knew you, before you were born I set you apart," said the LORD.

JEREMIAH 1:5

Do you not know that your body is a temple of the Holy Spirit, who is in you, whom you have received from God? You are not your own; you were bought at a price. Therefore honor God with your body.

1 CORINTHIANS 6:19–20

DEVOTIONAL THOUGHT ON IDENTITY

There is one area of my life—and yours—in which there is no need for competition. This truth comes through clearly in the words of Jeremiah's call: "Before you were born I set you apart" (Jeremiah 1:5). In other words, God was saying to this prophet, "You're a one of a kind, Jeremiah. I have no templates, no stencils. You can look around all you want, but you're the only man who is just like you."

Please do not miss this spellbinding truth: there is no competition in God's plan for you and me. His calling is as individualized as each person's fingerprint; it belongs to no one else.

Does this mean that before my parents had ever met, God had a specific work for me to accomplish? Yes, it does. And does this mean that if I want to discover the greatest joy in living, I need to take my focus away from others and tenaciously seek God's singular direction for me? Again, the answer is in the affirmative.

What has God called you to? Whatever it is, it's all yours. There's no wining or losing in this game … there's only obedience.

INTEGRITY

---

*In everything set ... an example by doing what is good.
In your teaching show integrity, seriousness and sound-
ness of speech that cannot be condemned.*

TITUS 2:7-8

The LORD ... delights in men who are truthful.

PROVERBS 12:22

*Blessed is the man who does not condemn himself by
what he approves.*

ROMANS 14:22

To do what is right and just
    is more acceptable to the LORD than sacrifice.

PROVERBS 21:3

Honest scales and balances are from the LORD;
    all the weights in the bag are of his making.

PROVERBS 16:11

*I put in charge of Jerusalem my brother Hanani, along
with Hananiah the commander of the citadel, because
he was a man of integrity and feared God more than
most men do.*

NEHEMIAH 7:2

INTEGRITY

———

We are taking pains to do what is right, not only in the eyes of the Lord but also in the eyes of men.

2 CORINTHIANS 8:21

Obey your earthly masters in everything; and do it, not only when their eye is on you and to win their favor, but with sincerity of heart and reverence for the Lord. Whatever you do, work at it with all your heart, as working for the Lord, not for men since you know that you will receive an inheritance from the Lord as a reward. It is the Lord Christ you are serving.

COLOSSIANS 3:22-24

The integrity of the upright guides them,
    but the unfaithful are destroyed
    by their duplicity.

PROVERBS 11:3

Make it your ambition to lead a quiet life, to mind your own business and to work with your hands, . . . so that your daily life may win the respect of outsiders and so that you will not be dependent on anybody.

1 THESSALONIANS 4:11-12

INTEGRITY

———

Live such good lives among [unbelievers] that, though they accuse you of doing wrong, they may see your good deeds and glorify God on the day he visits us.

1 PETER 2:12

Let the LORD judge the peoples.
Judge me, O LORD, according to my righteousness,
    according to my integrity, O Most High.

PSALM 7:8

The man of integrity walks securely,
    but he who takes crooked paths
    will be found out.

PROVERBS 10:9

God has showed you, O man, what is good.
    And what does the LORD require of you?
To act justly and to love mercy
    and to walk humbly with your God.

MICAH 6:8

I know, my God, that you test the heart and are pleased with integrity.

1 CHRONICLES 29:17

INTEGRITY

May integrity and uprightness protect me,
  because my hope is in you, O LORD.
Vindicate me, O LORD,
  for I have led a blameless life;
I have trusted in the LORD
  without wavering.
Test me, O LORD, and try me,
  examine my heart and my mind;
for your love is ever before me,
  and I walk continually in your truth.

PSALM 25:21, 26:1–3

Righteousness guards the man of integrity.

PROVERBS 13:6

The LORD takes the upright into his confidence.

PROVERBS 3:32

*I strive always to keep my conscience clear before God
and man.*

ACTS 24:16

INTEGRITY

Whatever is true, whatever is noble, whatever is right, whatever is pure, whatever is lovely, whatever is admirable—if anything is excellent or praiseworthy—think about such things.

PHILIPPIANS 4:8

Stand firm ... with the belt of truth buckled around your waist, with the breastplate of righteousness in place, and with your feet fitted with the readiness that comes from the gospel of peace.

EPHESIANS 6:14–15

DEVOTIONAL THOUGHT ON INTEGRITY

The apostle Paul declared, "I strive always to keep my conscience clear before God and man" (Acts 24:16). Imagine the courage, confidence, and self-assurance it took to say such a thing in the face of one's accusers.

What does it mean to have a clear conscience? It means that you can say with a straight face, "I have done everything I can do. There are no sins to confess. Look wherever you want, but there will be no surprises."

We are living in a time when men are quietly scrambling to hide from their pasts. Every day we hear of yet another man whose treacherous history is brought into the light of day.

Where are the Pauls? Where are the men who live with clear consciences? Do we live our lives just one small step ahead of the truth of our past, or do we rest because we've withheld no secrets?

You may have some confessions to submit … a record to clear up. There could be consequences. But my guess is that Paul would promise us that a soul vindicated from full disclosure is well worth any price we may have to pay. Regardless of the cost, it'll be worth it.

JOY

Light is shed upon the righteous
and joy on the upright in heart.

PSALM 97:11

The LORD will yet fill your mouth with laughter
and your lips with shouts of joy.

JOB 8:21

God's favor lasts a lifetime;
weeping may remain for a night,
but rejoicing comes in the morning.

PSALM 30:5

Rejoice in the LORD and be glad, you righteous;
sing, all you who are upright in heart!

PSALM 32:11

Let the righteous rejoice in the LORD
and take refuge in him;
let all the upright in heart praise him!

PSALM 64:10

Shout for joy to the LORD, all the earth.
Worship the LORD with gladness;
come before him with joyful songs.

PSALM 100:1-2

JOY

Jesus said, "As the Father has loved me, so have I loved you. Now remain in my love. If you obey my commands, you will remain in my love, just as I have obeyed my Father's commands and remain in his love. I have told you this so that my joy may be in you and that your joy may be complete."

JOHN 15:9–11

May all who seek you, O LORD,
 rejoice and be glad in you;
may those who love your salvation always say,
 "Let God be exalted!"

PSALM 70:4

The ransomed of the LORD will return.
 They will enter Zion with singing;
 everlasting joy will crown their heads.
Gladness and joy will overtake them,
 and sorrow and sighing will flee away.

ISAIAH 51:11

O God, let all who take refuge in you be glad;
 let them ever sing for joy.
Spread your protection over them,
 that those who love your name
 may rejoice in you.

PSALM 5:11

JOY

I rejoice in following your statutes, O LORD,
    as one rejoices in great riches.

PSALM 119:14

Those who sow in tears
    will reap with songs of joy.

PSALM 126:5

The prospect of the righteous is joy.

PROVERBS 10:28

You will go out in joy
    and be led forth in peace;
the mountains and hills
    will burst into song before you,
and all the trees of the field
    will clap their hands.

ISAIAH 55:12

Rejoice in the LORD your God,
for he has given you
    the autumn rains in righteousness.
He sends you abundant showers,
    both autumn and spring rains, as before.

JOEL 2:23

JOY

Jesus said, "Until now you have not asked for anything in my name. Ask and you will receive, and your joy will be complete."

JOHN 16:24

You have made known to me the paths of life, O Lord; you will fill me with joy in your presence.

ACTS 2:28

The kingdom of God is ... righteousness, peace and joy in the Holy Spirit.

ROMANS 14:17

Rejoice in the Lord always. I will say it again: Rejoice!

PHILIPPIANS 4:4

Be joyful always.

1 THESSALONIANS 5:16

May the God of hope fill you with all joy and peace as you trust in him, so that you may overflow with hope by the power of the Holy Spirit.

ROMANS 15:13

JOY

The joy of the LORD is your strength.

NEHEMIAH 8:10

The LORD has done great things for us,
and we are filled with joy.

PSALM 126:3

*Blessed are you when men hate you, when they exclude
you and insult you and reject your name as evil, because
of the Son of Man. Rejoice in that day and leap for joy,
because great is your reward in heaven.*

LUKE 6:22–23

The precepts of the LORD are right,
giving joy to the heart.
The commands of the LORD are radiant,
giving light to the eyes.

PSALM 19:8

Your statutes are my heritage forever, O LORD;
they are the joy of my heart.

PSALM 119:111

We wait in hope for the LORD;
he is our help and our shield.

JOY

In him our hearts rejoice,
for we trust in his holy name.

PSALM 33:20-21

I delight greatly in the LORD;
my soul rejoices in my God.
For he has clothed me with garments of salvation.

ISAIAH 61:10

My heart rejoices in the LORD; in the LORD my horn is lifted high.

1 SAMUEL 2:1

My soul glorifies the Lord and my spirit rejoices in God my Savior.

LUKE 1:46-47

You believe in Jesus Christ and are filled with an inexpressible and glorious joy.

1 PETER 1:8

Let us rejoice and be glad
and give him glory!
For the wedding of the Lamb has come,
and his bride has made herself ready.

REVELATION 19:7

JOY

I will rejoice in the LORD,
>   I will be joyful in God my Savior.
The Sovereign LORD is my strength;
>   he makes my feet like the feet of a deer,
>   he enables me to go on the heights.

HABAKKUK 3:18–19

One generation will commend your works
>   to another, O LORD;
>   they will tell of your mighty acts.
They will speak of the glorious splendor
>   of your majesty,
>   and I will meditate on your wonderful works.
They will tell of the power of your awesome works,
>   and I will proclaim your great deeds.
They will celebrate your abundant goodness
>   and joyfully sing of your righteousness.

PSALM 145:4–7

DEVOTIONAL THOUGHT ON JOY

The story of the Philippian jailer is one of the Bible's most remarkable stories of how God's grace can affect a father. Here was a man faced with the trauma of failure on the job. Jailers not only got fired when prisoners escaped; they often lost their lives as well. Following a midnight earthquake that turned the prison to rubble, the jailer was preparing to take his life. Paul and Silas shouted at the jailer, who was about to impale himself on his sword, "We are all here!" (Acts 16:28). Completely overwhelmed by this act of mercy, the jailer fell to his knees before his gracious captives. "Sirs," he cried, "what must I do to be saved?" (Acts 16:30).

That night, not only was the jailer brought into a relationship with God, but he also invited Paul and Silas to his home. As a result, the jailer "was filled with joy because he had come to believe in God—he and his whole family" (Acts 16:34).

Confess your sinfulness, enjoy his grace, then let your experience with Christ infect your family. Let it bring joy to your home.

KINDNESS

Good will come to him
who is generous and lends freely,
who conducts his affairs with justice.

PSALM 112:5

Blessed is he who is kind to the needy.

PROVERBS 14:21

Give to the one who asks you, and do not turn away from the one who wants to borrow from you.

MATTHEW 5:42

Jesus said, "Come, you who are blessed by my Father; take your inheritance, the kingdom prepared for you since the creation of the world. For I was hungry and you gave me something to eat, I was thirsty and you gave me something to drink, I was a stranger and you invited me in, I needed clothes and you clothed me, I was sick and you looked after me, I was in prison and you came to visit me."

MATTHEW 25:34–36

Love is kind.

1 CORINTHIANS 13:4

KINDNESS

Carry each other's burdens, and in this way you will fulfill the law of Christ.

GALATIANS 6:2

As we have opportunity, let us do good to all people.

GALATIANS 6:10

As God's chosen people, holy and dearly loved, clothe yourselves with compassion, kindness, humility, gentleness and patience.

COLOSSIANS 3:12

Make every effort to add to your faith ... brotherly kindness; and to brotherly kindness, love. For if you possess these qualities in increasing measure, they will keep you from being ineffective and unproductive in your knowledge of our Lord Jesus Christ.

2 PETER 1:5, 7–8

If anyone has material possessions and sees his brother in need but has no pity on him, how can the love of God be in him? Dear children, let us not love with words or tongue but with actions and in truth.

1 JOHN 3:17–18

KINDNESS

Ruth bowed down with her face to the ground. She exclaimed, "Why have I found such favor in your eyes that you notice me—a foreigner?" Boaz replied, "I've been told all about what you have done for your mother-in-law since the death of your husband—how you left your father and mother and your homeland and came to live with a people you did not know before. May the LORD repay you for what you have done. May you be richly rewarded by the LORD, the God of Israel, under whose wings you have come to take refuge."

RUTH 2:10–12

The fruit of the Spirit is love, joy, peace, patience, kindness, goodness, faithfulness.

GALATIANS 5:22

When the kindness and love of God our Savior appeared, he saved us, not because of righteous things we had done, but because of his mercy.

TITUS 3:4–5

Jesus said, "If anyone gives even a cup of cold water to one of these little ones because he is my disciple, I tell you the truth, he will certainly not lose his reward."

MATTHEW 10:42

DEVOTIONAL THOUGHT ON KINDNESS

———

Have you ever tried to sympathize with a child's scuffed knee without squatting down and stooping to his or her level? Of course, such a thing is impossible. Unless a child sees the understanding on your face, and unless he or she sees it down on his or her level, that child won't be able to accept your comfort.

The psalmist David saw that God demonstrated this kind of care for his children. David called it "compassion." God the Father takes moments from his busy schedule—keeping the stars and planets on their charted courses, growing food for a hungry world, or raising up and bringing down world leaders—to stoop to our level and have compassion on his bumped and bruised children.

You're a busy man. You've got places to go, people to see, deals to get done. But our busy heavenly Father, the Creator of the universe, has compassion. He's never too busy to stop, never too proud to stoop. It's a good thing, too. How else could we ever see his face?

Look carefully; this Father's got lots of love. He stops, then he stoops. I guess if he can do it, so can we.

LOVE

Jesus said, "Love each other as I have loved you."

JOHN 15:12

Be devoted to one another in brotherly love. Honor one another above yourselves.

ROMANS 12:10

Serve one another in love.

GALATIANS 5:13

You yourselves have been taught by God to love each other.

1 THESSALONIANS 4:9

How good and pleasant it is
    when brothers live together in unity!

PSALM 133:1

Live a life of love, just as Christ loved us and gave himself up for us as a fragrant offering and sacrifice to God.

EPHESIANS 5:2

May the Lord make your love increase and overflow for each other and for everyone else. . . .

1 THESSALONIANS 3:12

LOVE

Keep on loving each other.

HEBREWS 13:1

Live in harmony with one another; be sympathetic, love as brothers, be compassionate and humble.

1 PETER 3:8

Love does no harm to its neighbor. Therefore love is the fulfillment of the law.

ROMANS 13:10

Love ... comes from a pure heart and a good conscience and a sincere faith.

1 TIMOTHY 1:5

As God's chosen people, holy and dearly loved, clothe yourselves with compassion, kindness, humility, gentleness and patience. ... Over all these virtues put on love, which binds them all together in perfect unity.

COLOSSIANS 3:12, 14

Do everything in love.

1 CORINTHIANS 16:14

LOVE

Many waters cannot quench love;
  rivers cannot wash it away.
If one were to give
  all the wealth of his house for love,
  it would be utterly scorned.

SONG OF SONGS 8:7

Jesus said, "You have heard that it was said, 'Love your neighbor and hate your enemy.' But I tell you: Love your enemies and pray for those who persecute you."

MATTHEW 5:43-44

Let no debt remain outstanding, except the continuing debt to love one another, for he who loves his fellowman has fulfilled the law.

ROMANS 13:8

This is love: that we walk in obedience to God's commands. As you have heard from the beginning, his command is that you walk in love.

2 JOHN 6

How great is the love the Father has lavished on us, that we should be called children of God! And that is what we are!

1 JOHN 3:1

LOVE

Praise be to the LORD,
for he showed his wonderful love to me.

PSALM 31:21

O LORD, how priceless is your unfailing love!
Both high and low among men
find refuge in the shadow of your wings.

PSALM 36:7

I will sing of the LORD's great love forever;
with my mouth I will make
your faithfulness known
through all generations, O God.

PSALM 89:1

God demonstrates his own love for us in this: While we were still sinners, Christ died for us.

ROMANS 5:8

I pray that you, being rooted and established in love, may have power, together with all the saints, to grasp how wide and long and high and deep is the love of Christ.

EPHESIANS 3:17–18

LOVE

Let us love one another, for love comes from God. Everyone who loves has been born of God and knows God. Whoever does not love does not know God, because God is love.

1 JOHN 4:7-8

If I speak in the tongues of men and of angels, but have not love, I am only a resounding gong or a clanging cymbal. If I have the gift of prophecy and can fathom all mysteries and all knowledge, and if I have a faith that can move mountains, but have not love, I am nothing. If I give all I possess to the poor and surrender my body to the flames, but have not love, I gain nothing. Love is patient, love is kind. It does not envy, it does not boast, it is not proud. It is not rude, it is not self-seeking, it is not easily angered, it keeps no record of wrongs. Love does not delight in evil but rejoices with the truth. It always protects, always trusts, always hopes, always perseveres. Love never fails.

1 CORINTHIANS 13:1-8

The only thing that counts is faith expressing itself through love.

GALATIANS 5:6

LOVE

Because of his great love for us, God, who is rich in mercy, made us alive with Christ even when we were dead in transgressions.

EPHESIANS 2:4–5

This is love: not that we loved God, but that he loved us and sent his Son as an atoning sacrifice for our sins.

1 JOHN 4:10

Now that you have purified yourselves by obeying the truth so that you have sincere love for your brothers, love one another deeply, from the heart.

1 PETER 1:22

No one has ever seen God; but if we love one another, God lives in us and his love is made complete in us.

1 JOHN 4:12

God so loved the world that he gave his one and only Son, that whoever believes in him shall not perish but have eternal life.

JOHN 3:16

LOVE

This is how we know what love is: Jesus Christ laid down his life for us. And we ought to lay down our lives for our brothers.

1 JOHN 3:16

Love each other deeply, because love covers over a multitude of sins.

1 PETER 4:8

Devotional Thought on Love

We will hear the word love spoken today. We may even speak it ourselves. But lest we consign this word to a child's penny valentine or a whimpering teenager expressing himself in a love note, we cannot forget its unmistakable power.

The phrase "I love you" changed your life. Once you were a single man, free to move about at will; "I love you" inextricably bound you to one woman for the rest of your life. "I love you" gave you a child—a little person who relentlessly watches your every move, keeping you on the straight and narrow.

"I love you" opened our heavenly Father's hand to welcome us—sinful as we were—to himself. "I love you" gave us Jesus, who endured the cross for those sins.

"I love you" is about the serious stuff of life. Its impact changes people. Its power moves them away from their complacency. It alters their plans. It renders them speechless.

You love your family. Your family loves you. Love changes everything.

MARRIAGE

---

*Husbands ought to love their wives as their own bodies.
He who loves his wife loves himself. After all, no one
ever hated his own body, but he feeds and cares for it,
just as Christ does the church—for we are members of
his body. "For this reason a man will leave his father
and mother and be united to his wife, and the two will
become one flesh."*

EPHESIANS 5:28–31

Place me like a seal over your heart,
    like a seal on your arm;
for love is as strong as death,
    its jealousy unyielding as the grave.
It burns like blazing fire,
    like a mighty flame.
Many waters cannot quench love;
    rivers cannot wash it away.
If one were to give
    all the wealth of his house for love,
    it would be utterly scorned.

SONG OF SONGS 8:6–7

All beautiful you are, my darling;
    there is no flaw in you. ...
You have stolen my heart, my sister, my bride;
    you have stolen my heart

---

with one glance of your eyes,
    with one jewel of your necklace.
How delightful is your love, my sister, my bride!
    How much more pleasing is your
    love than wine,
    and the fragrance of your perfume
    than any spice!

SONG OF SONGS 4:7, 9-10

Enjoy life with your wife, whom you love. . . .

ECCLESIASTES 9:9

A wife of noble character who can find?
    She is worth far more than rubies.
Her husband has full confidence in her
    and lacks nothing of value.
She brings him good, not harm,
    all the days of her life.
Her children arise and call her blessed;
    her husband also, and he praises her:
"Many women do noble things,
    but you surpass them all."

PROVERBS 31:10-12, 28-29

MARRIAGE

Arise, my darling,
my beautiful one, and come with me.
See! The winter is past;
    the rains are over and gone.
Flowers appear on the earth;
    the season of singing has come,
the cooing of the doves
    is heard in our land.

SONG OF SONGS 2:10–12

DEVOTIONAL THOUGHT ON MARRIAGE

Do you remember your first love? Do you remember how you "accidentally" let your hand brush against hers, hoping she would not resist? Do you remember collecting the courage to kiss a girl for the first time? And how about the excitement of pursuing the woman who would one day become your wife?

Although the tender words of love you used to speak have been eclipsed by discussions about schedules, car pools and trash in the kitchen, your wife still needs the romance of your first embrace.

Do something today that takes you back to those days of grade-school love. Be daring. Lavish her with something she doesn't expect. You never know when the bell will ring and this golden opportunity will end. Recess never lasts long enough.

MONEY

He who gathers money little by little makes it grow.

PROVERBS 13:11

Wisdom is a shelter
     as money is a shelter,
but the advantage of knowledge is this:
     that wisdom preserves the life of its possessor.

ECCLESIASTES 7:12

Command those who are rich in this present world not to be arrogant nor to put their hope in wealth, which is so uncertain, but to put their hope in God, who richly provides us with everything for our enjoyment. Command them to do good, to be rich in good deeds, and to be generous and willing to share. In this way they will lay up treasure for themselves as a firm foundation for the coming age, so that they may take hold of the life that is truly life.

1 TIMOTHY 6:17–19

Jesus said, "No one can serve two masters. Either he will hate the one and love the other, or he will be devoted to the one and despise the other. You cannot serve both God and Money."

MATTHEW 6:24

MONEY

Jesus said, "Do not store up for yourselves treasures on earth, where moth and rust destroy, and where thieves break in and steal. But store up for yourselves treasures in heaven, where moth and rust do not destroy, and where thieves do not break in and steal."

MATTHEW 6:19–20

Keep your lives free from the love of money and be content with what you have.

HEBREWS 13:5

Remember the LORD your God, for it is he who gives you the ability to produce wealth, and so confirms his covenant, which he swore to your forefathers, as it is today.

DEUTERONOMY 8:18

God will meet all your needs according to his glorious riches in Christ Jesus.

PHILIPPIANS 4:19

Whoever can be trusted with very little can also be trusted with much. . . .

LUKE 16:10

MONEY

Turn my heart toward your statutes, O LORD,
and not toward selfish gain.

PSALM 119:36

*Use worldly wealth to gain friends for yourselves, so that
when it is gone, you will be welcomed into eternal
dwellings.*

LUKE 16:9

"Why spend money on what is not bread,
and your labor on what does not satisfy?
Listen, listen to me, and eat what is good,
and your soul will delight in the richest of fare,"
declares the LORD.

ISAIAH 55:2

DEVOTIONAL THOUGHT ON MONEY

Tithing is a word that means giving ten percent of our income to further God's work in the world. By tithing, we show God that we are thankful for the blessings he's given us. When we tithe, we also acknowledge that God owns everything we have anyway and that we want to honor him by giving some of that back to him.

Tithing is a part of God's plan to keep his church in order. Our tithes go to pay the staff's salary, cover the bills for the church, and help others who are needy. It's important to God that we honor him with our finances. Through the prophet Malachi, the Lord told the Israelites to tithe faithfully. "Test me in this," he said, "and see if I will not throw open the floodgates of heaven and pour out so much blessing that you will not have room enough for it" (Malachi 3:10).

And one more thing . . . we don't honor God so that he will honor us. We honor him because he's God, and he deserves it. Look at how he's already blessed you, then consider how much of what you own comes from God's hand.

OBEDIENCE

This is how we know that we love the children of God: by loving God and carrying out his commands. This is love for God: to obey his commands. And his commands are not burdensome.

1 JOHN 5:2–3

We will serve the LORD our God and obey him.

JOSHUA 24:24

God said, "If you walk in my ways and obey my statutes and commands ... I will give you a long life."

1 KINGS 3:14

I have considered my ways
    and have turned my steps
       to your statutes, O LORD.
I will hasten and not delay
    to obey your commands.

PSALM 119:59–60

Those who obey God's commands live in him, and he in them. And this is how we know that he lives in us: We know it by the Spirit he gave us.

1 JOHN 3:24

OBEDIENCE

All the ways of the LORD are loving and faithful
    for those who keep the demands
    of his covenant.

PSALM 25:10

I have kept my feet from every evil path
    so that I might obey your word, O LORD.

PSALM 119:101

From everlasting to everlasting
    the LORD's love is with those who fear him,
and his righteousness with
    their children's children—
with those who keep his covenant
    and remember to obey his precepts.

PSALM 103:17-18

*If anyone obeys God's word, God's love is truly made
complete in him.*

1 JOHN 2:5

Blessed are they who keep God's statutes
    and seek him with all their heart.
They do nothing wrong;
    they walk in his ways.

PSALM 119:2-3

OBEDIENCE

He who obeys instructions guards his life. ...

"Obey me, and I will be your God and you will be my people. Walk in all the ways I command you, that it may go well with you," says the LORD.

JEREMIAH 7:23

Jesus said, "If anyone loves me, he will obey my teaching. My Father will love him, and we will come to him and make our home with him."

JOHN 14:23

Obey your leaders and submit to their authority. They keep watch over you as men who must give an account. Obey them so that their work will be a joy, not a burden.

HEBREWS 13:17

To love God with all your heart, with all your understanding and with all your strength, and to love your neighbor as yourself is more important than all burnt offerings and sacrifices.

MARK 12:33

DEVOTIONAL THOUGHT ON
OBEDIENCE

———

God stepped up with what seemed like a cruel assignment. "Kill your boy," God told an astonished Abraham. "Sacrifice him to me." What an incomprehensible request! But Isaac's dad was willing to obey his heavenly Father, regardless of the message. He had acted in faith before, and he would do it again this time.

The story of Abraham's willingness to sacrifice his son is not only about the incredible tug of a dad's heart toward his child. It's also about a man who knew that obedience was more important than the potential losses incurred in the sacrifice.

The story of the Bible is filled with this principle: If you want to come into God's presence, everything else—even your most precious possession—has to be offered up to him. A second-stringer wasn't good enough. God was so adamant about this principle that he was willing to lay his own unblemished Son on the altar.

Abraham is a great example for us. He would have wanted us to learn, too: God must be first; when I hear his voice, I must obey. Nothing else really matters.

PATIENCE

I wait for the LORD, my soul waits,
    and in his word I put my hope.
My soul waits for the LORD
    more than watchmen wait for the morning.

PSALM 130:5-6

Be still before the LORD and wait patiently for him.

PSALM 37:7

*Everyone should be quick to listen, slow to speak and
slow to become angry.*

JAMES 1:19

Patience is better than pride.

ECCLESIASTES 7:8

It is good to wait quietly
    for the salvation of the LORD.

LAMENTATIONS 3:26

Wait for the LORD;
    be strong and take heart
    and wait for the LORD.

PSALM 27:14

LORD, walking in the way of your laws,
    we wait for you;

PATIENCE

your name and renown
     are the desire of our hearts.

ISAIAH 26:8

Be joyful in hope, patient in affliction, faithful in prayer.

ROMANS 12:12

If we hope for what we do not yet have, we wait for it patiently.

ROMANS 8:25

See how the farmer waits for the land to yield its valuable crop and how patient he is for the autumn and spring rains. You too, be patient and stand firm, because the Lord's coming is near.

JAMES 5:7–8

Love is patient.

1 CORINTHIANS 13:4

Be completely humble and gentle; be patient, bearing with one another in love.

EPHESIANS 4:2

PATIENCE

We pray ... that you may live a life worthy of the Lord and may please him in every way: bearing fruit in every good work, growing in the knowledge of God, being strengthened with all power according to his glorious might so that you may have great endurance and patience.

COLOSSIANS 1:10–11

Pursue righteousness, godliness, faith, love, endurance and gentleness.

1 TIMOTHY 6:11

You, O LORD, are a compassionate
    and gracious God,
        slow to anger, abounding in love
        and faithfulness.

PSALM 86:15

The Lord is not slow in keeping his promise, as some understand slowness. He is patient with you, not wanting anyone to perish, but everyone to come to repentance.

2 PETER 3:9

DEVOTIONAL THOUGHT ON PATIENCE

Wouldn't it be great if we could read from Noah's nautical journal? Day 1 might have read, "God, you really did keep your word. Thank you for giving me the strength to obey. Thank you for being so faithful." But day 173 may have read a bit differently. "Okay, God, I've had enough. This is the most miserable experience of my life. Are you there? Are you listening to me?"

Have you been there? Have you done something radical—moved your family to a new town or changed jobs—sincerely believing it was what God wanted you to do, only to find yourself completely miserable? I've been there, too.

Well, we're in good company—Noah, Abraham, Jacob, David, Job. These were men who heard God's voice, believed the promise, then had to wait. And wait. And wait some more.

Are you waiting for something you thought God would have delivered by now—satisfaction at work, healing from an illness, reconciliation with a friend? The assurance we have from the Bible is that, in every case, in his own way, God's promise was good. Those who had to wait did not wait in vain. Take that promise with you today.

PEACE

May the Lord of peace himself give you peace at all times and in every way. The Lord be with all of you.

2 THESSALONIANS 3:16

LORD, you establish peace for us;
    all that we have accomplished you have done for us.

ISAIAH 26:12

Let the peace of Christ rule in your hearts, since as members of one body you were called to peace.

COLOSSIANS 3:15

Do not be anxious about anything, but in everything, by prayer and petition, with thanksgiving, present your requests to God. And the peace of God, which transcends all understanding, will guard your hearts and your minds in Christ Jesus.

PHILIPPIANS 4:6–7

I will lie down and sleep in peace,
    for you alone, O LORD,
      make me dwell in safety.

PSALM 4:8

GOD'S WORDS OF LIFE ON

PEACE

The LORD gives strength to his people;
  the LORD blesses his people with peace.

PSALM 29:11

O LORD, you will keep in perfect peace
  him whose mind is steadfast,
  because he trusts in you.

ISAIAH 26:3

Great peace have they who love your law, O LORD,
  and nothing can make them stumble.

PSALM 119:165

To us a child is born,
  to us a son is given,
  and the government will be on his shoulders.
And he will be called
  Wonderful Counselor, Mighty God,
  Everlasting Father, Prince of Peace.

ISAIAH 9:6

*Grace and peace to you from God our Father and the
Lord Jesus Christ.*

PHILIPPIANS 1:2

PEACE

God said, "I will make a covenant of peace with them and rid the land of wild beasts so that they may live in the desert and sleep in the forests in safety. I will bless them and the places surrounding my hill. I will send down showers in season; there will be showers of blessing. The trees of the field will yield their fruit and the ground will yield its crops; the people will be secure in their land. They will know that I am the LORD."

EZEKIEL 34:25–27

You know the message God sent to the people of Israel, telling the good news of peace through Jesus Christ, who is Lord of all.

ACTS 10:36

The LORD bless you
and keep you;
the LORD make his face shine upon you
and be gracious to you;
the LORD turn his face toward you
and give you peace.

NUMBERS 6:24–26

Grace and peace to you from God who is, and who was, and who is to come.

REVELATION 1:4

PEACE

Love and faithfulness meet together;
   righteousness and peace kiss each other.

PSALM 85:10

This is what the LORD says:
"I will extend peace to her like a river,
   and the wealth of nations
   like a flooding stream."

ISAIAH 66:12

*Make every effort to keep the unity of the Spirit through
the bond of peace.*

EPHESIANS 4:3

*If it is possible, as far as it depends on you, live at peace
with everyone.*

ROMANS 12:18

*Peacemakers who sow in peace raise a harvest of right-
eousness.*

JAMES 3:18

*Jesus said, "Peace I leave with you; my peace I give you.
I do not give to you as the world gives. Do not let your
hearts be troubled and do not be afraid."*

JOHN 14:27

PEACE

Blessed are the peacemakers, for they will be called sons of God.

MATTHEW 5:9

Let us therefore make every effort to do what leads to peace and to mutual edification.

ROMANS 14:19

Submit to God and be at peace with him;
    in this way prosperity will come to you.

JOB 22:21

The fruit of righteousness will be peace;
    the effect of righteousness will be
    quietness and confidence forever.

ISAIAH 32:17

Devotional Thought on Peace

As the doors slid open to the terminal, I felt great. I was ready for this business trip, whatever surprises it threw my way. I felt great.

In less than sixty seconds, I was standing at the metal detectors. I loaded my small suitcase and briefcase onto the conveyor belt. Once they had disappeared into the X-ray machine, I stepped through the electronic trellis.

A security officer stopped me. "You got a computer in there?" he asked. "Uh, yes I do," I responded, trying to keep my composure. "Turn it on for me," he ordered.

Standing there, waiting for my laptop to boot up, I felt myself filling with rage. I got mad at all this airport security; I got mad at the X-ray police; I got mad at my laptop that booted up so slowly.

By the time the security checks were complete, I was furious. The peace I had felt when I had entered the airport was a distant memory. I was looking for something to kick.

The next time you get derailed, take confidence in the good stuff you've put into your soul. God's holy presence is yours. He will calm you down.

PLANNING

Plans fail for lack of counsel,
    but with many advisers they succeed.

PROVERBS 15:22

The plans of the righteous are just.

PROVERBS 12:5

O LORD, I know that you can do all things;
    no plan of yours can be thwarted.

JOB 42:2

    The LORD Almighty has sworn,
"Surely, as I have planned, so it will be,
    and as I have purposed, so it will stand."

ISAIAH 14:24

Those who plan what is good find love and
faithfulness.

PROVERBS 14:22

The plans of the diligent lead to profit
    as surely as haste leads to poverty.

PROVERBS 21:5

The noble man makes noble plans,
    and by noble deeds he stands.

ISAIAH 32:8

PLANNING

Make plans by seeking advice.

PROVERBS 20:18

You who say, "Today or tomorrow we will go to this or that city, spend a year there, carry on business and make money." Why, you do not even know what will happen tomorrow. What is your life? You are a mist that appears for a little while and then vanishes. Instead, you ought to say, "If it is the Lord's will, we will live and do this or that."

JAMES 4:13-15

The LORD foils the plans of the nations;
    he thwarts the purposes of the peoples.
But the plans of the LORD stand firm forever,
    the purposes of his heart through all
    generations.

PSALM 33:10-11

May the LORD give you the desire of your heart
    and make all your plans succeed.

PSALM 20:4

Many are the plans in a man's heart,
    but it is the LORD's purpose that prevails.

PROVERBS 19:21

PLANNING

To man belong the plans of the heart,
  but from the Lord comes the reply
  of the tongue.

All a man's ways seem innocent to him,
  but motives are weighed by the LORD.
Commit to the LORD whatever you do,
  and your plans will succeed.

PROVERBS 16:1–3

There is no wisdom, no insight, no plan
  that can succeed against the LORD.

PROVERBS 21:30

DEVOTIONAL THOUGHT ON PLANNING

Most men I know carry some kind of calendar. The one I carry is huge. It includes places for my license and credit cards along with monthly and daily calendars. This is sound planning, wouldn't you agree? Come to think of it, it's pretty presumptuous too.

Although King Solomon never carried a planner or attended a time-management seminar, he certainly understood all of these things. "Do not boast about tomorrow, for you do not know what a day may bring forth," he wisely said (Proverbs 27:1).

My grandmother took this exhortation seriously. She never talked about future plans without prefacing them with, "The Lord willing." "The Lord willing, we'll have roasted chicken for dinner." "The Lord willing, we'll go to the store tomorrow." "The Lord willing, we'll see you this summer."

Carrying a calendar is good. Planning is a wise use of your time. Knowing what's coming next week, next month, and next year makes a lot of sense. But be sure to write this stuff in pencil, and be careful about being too confident. The Lord willing, we'll get to tomorrow.

POWER

Jesus said, "With God all things are possible."

MATTHEW 19:26

I am the LORD, the God of all mankind. Is anything too hard for me?

JEREMIAH 32:27

The LORD is slow to anger and great in power;
>   the LORD will not leave the guilty unpunished.
His way is in the whirlwind and the storm,
>   and clouds are the dust of his feet.

NAHUM 1:3

All the peoples of the earth
>   are regarded as nothing.
God does as he pleases
>   with the powers of heaven
>   and the peoples of the earth.
No one can hold back his hand
>   or say to him: "What have you done?"

DANIEL 4:35

You are awesome, O God, in your sanctuary;
>   the God of Israel gives power
>   and strength to his people.
Praise be to God!

PSALM 68:35

POWER

Your strength will equal your days.

DEUTERONOMY 33:25

"I will strengthen them in the LORD
and in his name they will walk,"
declares the LORD.

ZECHARIAH 10:12

*We pray ... that you may live a life worthy of the Lord
and may please him in every way: bearing fruit in
every good work, growing in the knowledge of God,
being strengthened with all power according to his glorious might so that you may have great endurance and
patience.*

COLOSSIANS 1:10–11

The LORD spreads out the northern skies
over empty space;
he suspends the earth over nothing.
He wraps up the waters in his clouds,
yet the clouds do not burst under their weight.
He covers the face of the full moon,
spreading his clouds over it.
He marks out the horizon on the face of the waters
for a boundary between light and darkness. ...
By his breath the skies became fair;

POWER

---

his hand pierced the gliding serpent.
And these are but the outer fringe of God's works;
how faint the whisper we hear of him!
Who then can understand the thunder of his power?

JOB 26:7-11, 13-14

*God has made everything beautiful in its time. He has
also set eternity in the hearts of men; yet they cannot
fathom what God has done from beginning to end.*

ECCLESIASTES 3:11

God's wisdom is profound, his power is vast.
Who has resisted him and come out unscathed?

JOB 9:4

Your arm is endued with power, O LORD;
your hand is strong, your right hand exalted.

PSALM 89:13

Your right hand, O LORD,
was majestic in power.
Your right hand, O LORD,
shattered the enemy.

EXODUS 15:6

Be strong in the Lord and in his mighty power.

EPHESIANS 6:10

POWER

Yours, O LORD, is the greatness and the power
    and the glory and the majesty and the splendor,
      for everything in heaven and earth is yours.
Yours, O LORD, is the kingdom;
    you are exalted as head over all.
Wealth and honor come from you;
    you are the ruler of all things.
In your hands are strength and power
    to exalt and give strength to all.
Now, our God, we give you thanks,
    and praise your glorious name.

1 CHRONICLES 29:11–13

*I pray that out of God's glorious riches he may
strengthen you with power through his Spirit in your
inner being, so that Christ may dwell in your hearts
through faith. And I pray that you, being rooted and
established in love, may have power, together with all
the saints, to grasp how wide and long and high and
deep is the love of Christ.*

EPHESIANS 3:16–18

As for me, I am filled with power,
    with the Spirit of the LORD,
    and with justice and might.

MICAH 3:8

POWER

Jesus said, "You will receive power when the Holy Spirit comes on you; and you will be my witnesses in Jerusalem, and in all Judea and Samaria, and to the ends of the earth."

ACTS 1:8

"You may say to yourself, "My power and the strength of my hands have produced this wealth for me." But remember the LORD your God, for it is he who gives you the ability to produce wealth, and so confirms his covenant."

DEUTERONOMY 8:17–18

"Not by might nor by power, but by my Spirit," says the LORD Almighty.

ZECHARIAH 4:6

DEVOTIONAL THOUGHT ON POWER

How fast will your car go? You don't know? Well, how high do the numbers on your speedometer go—one hundred thirty … one forty … one fifty? And you've probably never even approached one hundred. Right? Wow, just think of all that raw unused power!

If you're mechanically inclined, you know something about this power. You know that if you actually drove at those speeds very often, you could cause serious damage to your engine.

In your job as a dad, you have a high-powered disciplinary engine with its own imaginary speedometer. This instrument registers numbers much higher than posted and safe speed limits. Do you have the right to push your accelerator to the floor and demonstrate some of that power? Of course you do.

But most experts agree that if you spend too much time at those high speeds, you'll do damage to yourself, not to mention those around you.

Sometimes dads are called upon to use their power. Yet even when you could use that power, it's usually better to hold back, leaving some of that brute force unused.

God's restraint—his mercy and his grace—is what makes him so awesome. His tenderness and patience melts our defiance and realigns our wayward hearts.

Perhaps you need to discover the power of unused power. Your family will be grateful.

PRAYER

"Before they call I will answer;
while they are still speaking I will hear,"
    says the LORD.

ISAIAH 65:24

*Ask and it will be given to you; seek and you will find;
knock and the door will be opened to you. For everyone
who asks receives; he who seeks finds; and to him who
knocks, the door will be opened.*

MATTHEW 7:7–8

*Jesus said, "I tell you that if two of you on earth agree
about anything you ask for, it will be done for you by
my Father in heaven. For where two or three come
together in my name, there am I with them."*

MATTHEW 18:19–20

*Dear friends, if our hearts do not condemn us, we have
confidence before God and receive from him anything
we ask, because we obey his commands and do what
pleases him.*

1 JOHN 3:21–22

Pray continually.

1 THESSALONIANS 5:17

PRAYER

The LORD is near to all who call on him,
     to all who call on him in truth.

PSALM 145:18

I call to God,
     and the LORD saves me.
Evening, morning and noon
     I cry out in distress,
     and he hears my voice.

PSALM 55:16–17

*When you pray, go into your room, close the door and
pray to your Father, who is unseen. Then your Father,
who sees what is done in secret, will reward you.*

MATTHEW 6:6

*Devote yourselves to prayer, being watchful and
thankful.*

COLOSSIANS 4:2

*"You will call upon me and come and pray to me, and
I will listen to you. You will seek me and find me when
you seek me with all your heart. I will be found by
you," declares the LORD.*

JEREMIAH 29:12–14

PRAYER

We have not stopped praying for you and asking God to fill you with the knowledge of his will through all spiritual wisdom and understanding.

COLOSSIANS 1:9

Pray in the Spirit on all occasions with all kinds of prayers and requests. With this in mind, be alert and always keep on praying for all the saints.

EPHESIANS 6:18

Let everyone who is godly pray to you, O LORD,
    while you may be found;
surely when the mighty waters rise,
    they will not reach him.

PSALM 32:6

Hear, O LORD, my righteous plea;
    listen to my cry.
Give ear to my prayer—
    it does not rise from deceitful lips.

PSALM 17:1

The LORD has heard my cry for mercy;
    the LORD accepts my prayer.

PSALM 6:9

Prayer

"Call to me and I will answer you and tell you great and unsearchable things you do not know," says the LORD.

JEREMIAH 33:3

"Because he loves me," says the LORD,
  "I will rescue him;
  I will protect him,
  for he acknowledges my name.
He will call upon me, and I will answer him;
  I will be with him in trouble,
  I will deliver him and honor him."

PSALM 91:14–15

The LORD is far from the wicked
  but he hears the prayer of the righteous.

PROVERBS 15:29

Delight yourself in the LORD
  and he will give you the desires of your heart.

PSALM 37:4

Let us ... approach the throne of grace with confidence, so that we may receive mercy and find grace to help us in our time of need.

HEBREWS 4:16

PRAYER

Jesus said, "I tell you the truth, my Father will give you whatever you ask in my name. Until now you have not asked for anything in my name. Ask and you will receive, and your joy will be complete."

JOHN 16:23–24

"If my people, who are called by my name, will humble themselves and pray and seek my face and turn from their wicked ways, then will I hear from heaven and will forgive their sin and will heal their land," says the Lord.

2 CHRONICLES 7:14

The eyes of the Lord are on the righteous
and his ears are attentive to their prayer.

1 PETER 3:12

Devotional Thought on Prayer

God spoke about Job to Satan, saying, "There is no one on earth like him; he is blameless and upright, a man who fears God and shuns evil" (Job 1:8). Perhaps one of the things that so impressed God about this man was the way he faithfully prayed for his children.

How often do your children see you face the altar and plead their case? "Father in heaven, please protect Missy today in school. Guard her mind and her actions. Talk to her through her friends who love you, and keep her from those who would turn her away from your love."

As Missy hears her dad hold her up before the throne of God, the chills run down her spine. My dad is praying for me. These words will roll over and over again in her mind. Over the course of the years, these prayers could change her life.

Pray for your children. Lift them up before the Father and seek his protection and blessing on their lives. This will be a powerful thing—both for you and for them.

PRIORITIES

Since we are surrounded by such a great cloud of witnesses, let us throw off everything that hinders and the sin that so easily entangles, and let us run with perseverance the race marked out for us. Let us fix our eyes on Jesus, the author and perfecter of our faith, who for the joy set before him endured the cross, scorning its shame, and sat down at the right hand of the throne of God.

HEBREWS 12:1–2

Make my joy complete by being like-minded, having the same love, being one in spirit and purpose. Do nothing out of selfish ambition or vain conceit, but in humility consider others better than yourselves. Each of you should look not only to your own interests, but also to the interests of others. Your attitude should be the same as that of Christ Jesus.

PHILIPPIANS 2:2–5

Jesus said, "This, then, is how you should pray: 'Our Father in heaven, hallowed be your name, your kingdom come, your will be done on earth as it is in heaven.'"

MATTHEW 6:9–10

PRIORITIES

———

Whatever was to my profit I now consider loss for the sake of Christ. What is more, I consider everything a loss compared to the surpassing greatness of knowing Christ Jesus my Lord, for whose sake I have lost all things. I consider them rubbish, that I may gain Christ.

PHILIPPIANS 3:7–8

I consider my life worth nothing to me, if only I may finish the race and complete the task the Lord Jesus has given me—the task of testifying to the gospel of God's grace.

ACTS 20:24

Jesus said, "Do not worry, saying, 'What shall we eat?' or 'What shall we drink?' or 'What shall we wear?'"... Seek first his kingdom and his righteousness, and all these things will be given to you as well."

MATTHEW 6:31, 33

Jesus said, "I tell you, use worldly wealth to gain friends for yourselves, so that when it is gone, you will be welcomed into eternal dwellings. Whoever can be trusted with very little can also be trusted with much, and whoever is dishonest with very little will also be dishonest with much. So if you have not been trustworthy in

PRIORITIES

handling worldly wealth, who will trust you with true riches?"

LUKE 16:9–11

Blessed is the man
    who does not walk in the counsel of the wicked
or stand in the way of sinners
    or sit in the seat of mockers.
But his delight is in the law of the LORD,
    and on his law he meditates day and night.

PSALM 1:1–2

Someone will say, "You have faith; I have deeds." Show me your faith without deeds, and I will show you my faith by what I do.

JAMES 2:18

Whatever you do, work at it with all your heart, as working for the Lord, not for men, since you know that you will receive an inheritance from the Lord as a reward. It is the Lord Christ you are serving.

COLOSSIANS 3:23–24

DEVOTIONAL THOUGHT ON PRIORITIES

———

I am a card-carrying acrophobic; I'm desperately afraid of heights.

I was building a house with my Sunday school class. Since I'm fairly adept at driving nails, I had volunteered to climb up to the top of the first floor framed walls to secure them.

When I had completed one section, I stood to walk across the three-and-a-half-inch wide "walkway" to the other side of the house. Suddenly, my legs froze. I could feel the pounding of my heart from my fingertips to my baseball cap. This was not funny.

Without looking up or down, I slowly reached my arms straight out from my sides and began to walk … one treacherous step at a time. Halfway across, I realized that my outstretched arms were providing the perfect antidote for my fear—they were giving me balance.

Being successful at work, effectively fathering your kids, keeping your exercise and diet routine intact, spending enough time with your wife, being disciplined in your spiritual life, … all of this can create such anxiety that you feel frozen, unable to walk across the high wall. How does one achieve balance in life?

Throughout his life Jesus kept his priorities in order, He refused to allow the stress and pressure of any one of the [obligations of life] to overshadow the others. Then one dark Friday afternoon, our Savior spread out his arms and gave his life for you and me. His provision of grace provided us with the luxury of living our lives in perfect balance—unencumbered by the relentless pressures of life. Isn't this incredible?

SELF-CONTROL

Surely you desire truth in the inner parts, O Lord;
　　you teach me wisdom in the inmost place.

PSALM 51:6

*The world and its desires pass away, but the man who
does the will of God lives forever.*

1 JOHN 2:17

The mind controlled by the Spirit is life and peace.

ROMANS 8:6

*Do your best to present yourself to God as one approved,
a workman who does not need to be ashamed.*

2 TIMOTHY 2:15

The fruit of righteousness will be peace
　　the effect of righteousness will be
　　quietness and confidence forever.

ISAIAH 32:17

O LORD, you will keep in perfect peace
　　him whose mind is steadfast
　　because he trusts in you.

ISAIAH 26:3

SELF-CONTROL

The kingdom of God is not a matter of eating and drinking, but of righteousness, peace and joy in the Holy Spirit.

ROMANS 14:17

Since ... you have been raised with Christ, set your hearts on things above, where Christ is seated at the right hand of God. Set your minds on things above, not on earthly things.

COLOSSIANS 3:1–2

Be careful, and watch yourselves closely so that you do not forget the things your eyes have seen or let them slip from your heart as long as you live. Teach them to your children and to their children after them.

DEUTERONOMY 4:9

Let your eyes look straight ahead,
　　fix your gaze directly before you.
Make level paths for your feet
　　and take only ways that are firm.
Do not swerve to the right or the left;
　　keep your foot from evil.

PROVERBS 4:25–27

SELF-CONTROL

*This is my prayer: that your love may abound more
and more in knowledge and depth of insight, so that
you may be able to discern what is best and may be
pure and blameless until the day of Christ.*

PHILIPPIANS 1:9-10

*Jesus said, "Whoever finds his life will lose it, and who-
ever loses his life for my sake will find it."*

MATTHEW 10:39

He follows my decrees
    and faithfully keeps my laws.
That man is righteous;
    he will surely live,
    declares the Sovereign LORD.

EZEKIEL 18:9

*The grace of God that brings salvation has appeared to
all men. It teaches us to say "No" to ungodliness and
worldly passions, and to live self-controlled, upright
and godly lives in this present age.*

TITUS 2:11-12

DEVOTIONAL THOUGHT ON SELF-CONTROL

Exodus 20–23 contains a list of pretty tough rules for the Israelites to follow. I'm sure listening to this list was as stressful to these people as getting ready for finals in school was for us. As we're getting down toward the end of the list of laws, we bump into something pretty simple—and powerful. Something that sounds as if it could have been written for my college experience: Do not follow the crowd in doing wrong (Exodus 23:2).

As adults, the pull toward doing wrong because our entire culture seems to be doing it—shaving the truth just a bit, saying regretful things, the temptation toward moral failure—is pretty overwhelming. And of course, our children face this terrible temptation, as well.

So what's the Bible's persuasive advice for this dilemma? It's a simple "don't." No explanation necessary. Just "don't." The writer of these words knew what we know. Following a crowd to do wrong things is stupid. So don't do it. Set an example for your family and stand for what you know is right. Encourage your kids to do the same. You'll both be so happy you did.

SERVANTHOOD

Whoever wants to become great among you must be your servant, and whoever wants to be first must be slave of all.

MARK 10:43-44

Though I am free and belong to no man, I make myself a slave to everyone, to win as many as possible. To the Jews I became like a Jew, to win the Jews. To those under the law I became like one under the law (though I myself am not under the law), so as to win those under the law. To those not having the law I became like one not having the law (though I am not free from God's law but am under Christ's law), so as to win those not having the law. To the weak I became weak, to win the weak. I have become all things to all men so that by all possible means I might save some.

1 CORINTHIANS 9:19-22

Your attitude should be the same as that of Christ Jesus: Who, being in very nature God, did not consider equality with God something to be grasped, but made himself nothing, taking the very nature of a servant, being made in human likeness. And being found in

---

appearance as a man, he humbled himself and became obedient to death—even death on a cross!

PHILIPPIANS 2:5–8

Jesus said, "Whoever wants to save his life will lose it, but whoever loses his life for me will find it."

MATTHEW 16:25

If serving the LORD seems undesirable to you, then choose for yourselves this day whom you will serve. ... as for me and my household, we will serve the LORD.

JOSHUA 24:15

Be devoted to one another in brotherly love. Honor one another above yourselves. Never be lacking in zeal, but keep your spiritual fervor, serving the Lord.

ROMANS 12:10–11

What does the LORD your God ask of you but to fear the LORD your God, to walk in all his ways, to love him, to serve the LORD your God with all your heart and with all your soul, and to observe the LORD's commands and decrees.

DEUTERONOMY 10:12–13

SERVANTHOOD

Be sure to fear the LORD and serve him faithfully with all your heart; consider what great things he has done for you.

1 SAMUEL 12:24

Jesus told his disciples, "Whoever welcomes this little child in my name welcomes me; and whoever welcomes me welcomes the one who sent me. For he who is least among you all—he is the greatest."

LUKE 9:48

If anyone serves, he should do it with the strength God provides, so that in all things God may be praised through Jesus Christ. To him be the glory and the power for ever and ever. Amen.

1 PETER 4:11

Serve one another in love.

GALATIANS 5:13

DEVOTIONAL THOUGHT ON SERVANTHOOD

The setting of the Last Supper was very informal, contrary to the many artists' renditions of the scene. These men were celebrating the Passover in the traditional way, reclining on the floor.

Suddenly Jesus stood up, took off his outer robe, tied a towel around his waist, poured water into a basin, and began washing his disciples' filthy feet. Here was the long-hoped-for Messiah, the Savior of mankind, on his knees, rinsing road dirt. *Where's the house boy?* they must have thought to themselves. Jesus shouldn't be doing this!

So what was Jesus doing? What was he "saying" in this moment of subservient humility? Love requires humility—power demands service.

Do we want respect at home? Of course we do. Do we want to own up to our responsibility as the "head of our homes"? Absolutely. Then we have to trade in our professional uniform for a work shirt, our crown for a basin, our robe for a towel. We're going to have to get off our high horse and get on our knees. Confessing. Washing. Forgiving. Serving. Jesus' example on this unforgettable night ought to be enough.

SPIRITUAL GROWTH

Forgetting what is behind and straining toward what is ahead, I press on toward the goal to win the prize for which God has called me heavenward in Christ Jesus.

PHILIPPIANS 3:13–14

Jesus said, "Whoever believes in me, as the Scripture has said, streams of living water will flow from within him."

JOHN 7:38

We will no longer be infants, tossed back and forth by the waves, and blown here and there by every wind of teaching and by the cunning and craftiness of men in their deceitful scheming. Instead, speaking the truth in love, we will in all things grow up into him who is the Head, that is, Christ. From him the whole body, joined and held together by every supporting ligament, grows and builds itself up in love, as each part does its work.

EPHESIANS 4:14–16

The fruit of the Spirit is love, joy, peace, patience, kindness, goodness, faithfulness, gentleness and self-control. Against such things there is no law. Those who belong to Christ Jesus have crucified the sinful nature with its

SPIRITUAL GROWTH

---

passions and desires. Since we live by the Spirit, let us keep in step with the Spirit.

GALATIANS 5:22-25

Those who live in accordance with the Spirit have their minds set on what the Spirit desires.

ROMANS 8:5

A time is coming and has now come when the true worshipers will worship the Father in spirit and truth, for they are the kind of worshipers the Father seeks. God is spirit, and his worshipers must worship in spirit and in truth.

JOHN 4:23-24

I urge you, brothers, in view of God's mercy, to offer your bodies as living sacrifices, holy and pleasing to God—this is your spiritual act of worship.

ROMANS 12:1

Like newborn babies, crave pure spiritual milk, so that by it you may grow up in your salvation, now that you have tasted that the Lord is good.

1 PETER 2:2-3

SPIRITUAL GROWTH

———

Since we are receiving a kingdom that cannot be shaken, let us be thankful, and so worship God acceptably with reverence and awe.

HEBREWS 12:28

Let me understand the teaching of your precepts;
   then I will meditate on your wonders.

PSALM 119:27

Grow in the grace and knowledge of our Lord and Savior Jesus Christ. To him be glory both now and forever!

2 PETER 3:18

DEVOTIONAL THOUGHT ON
SPIRITUAL GROWTH

When I was in grade school, Memorial Day was my favorite holiday because I played in the marching band, and school was almost over for the whole summer. Now that I'm older, I still have a deep love for the day ... but for different reasons. It's humbling to realize that people—total strangers—spilled their blood for me.

God's people had a similar event in their tradition. God's promises had been so visible to the Jews that, every year, they set a week aside to remember and be grateful. This Jewish tradition has very, very important lesson to teach dads. You are the priest in your home. Tell your children about God's faithfulness. Introduce your loved ones to God's amazing grace. Bring your family to their own personal experience of saving faith.

We have no choice but to live our lives as an example. We must teach our children God's ways, remind them of his faithfulness, and show them his grace.

STRENGTH

The LORD gives strength to his people;
    the LORD blesses his people with peace.

PSALM 29:11

"I will strengthen them in the LORD
    and in his name they will walk,"
        declares the LORD.

ZECHARIAH 10:12

We pray ... in order that you may live a life worthy of the Lord and may please him in every way: bearing fruit in every good work, growing in the knowledge of God, being strengthened with all power according to his glorious might so that you may have great endurance.

COLOSSIANS 1:10–11

Even youths grow tired and weary,
    and young men stumble and fall;
but those who hope in the LORD
    will renew their strength.
They will soar on wings like eagles;
    they will run and not grow weary,
    they will walk and not be faint.

ISAIAH 40:30–31

STRENGTH

You are awesome, O God, in your sanctuary;
>   the God of Israel gives power
>   and strength to his people.
Praise be to God!

PSALM 68:35

The Lord said to me, "My grace is sufficient for you, for
my power is made perfect in weakness." Therefore I will
boast all the more gladly about my weaknesses, so that
Christ's power may rest on me. That is why, for Christ's
sake, I delight in weaknesses, in insults, in hardships, in
persecutions, in difficulties. For when I am weak, then
I am strong.

2 CORINTHIANS 12:9–10

The LORD is the strength of his people,
>   a fortress of salvation for his anointed one.

PSALM 28:8

In the LORD alone
>   are righteousness and strength.

ISAIAH 45:24

Be strong in the Lord and in his mighty power.

EPHESIANS 6:10

STRENGTH

God gives strength to the weary
and increases the power of the weak.

ISAIAH 40:29

*I pray that out of God's glorious riches he may
strengthen you with power through his Spirit in your
inner being.*

EPHESIANS 3:16

"I will strengthen you and help you;
I will uphold you with my
righteous right hand,"
says the LORD.

ISAIAH 41:10

*I can do everything through Christ who gives me
strength.*

PHILIPPIANS 4:13

*The eyes of the LORD range throughout the earth to
strengthen those whose hearts are fully committed
to him.*

2 CHRONICLES 16:9

DEVOTIONAL THOUGHT ON STRENGTH

You can't play a videotape in a compact disc player. If you want a certain result, you're going to have to be plugged into the right source.

Being a man who lives in such a way that your friends and your family are actually blessed because of your life is a very, very tall order. In fact, Jesus was quick to say that if we're not connected to him, our "fruit" will be worthless and our "branch" will die (John 15). And dead branches are only good for bonfires.

This principle isn't very deep. We all know that if we're not connecting ourselves to the right stuff, our disobedient lives will show it. We can't expect to fill our lives with sin and have others see purity and right-eousness. As computer programmers sometimes say, "Garbage in, garbage out."

If, in the quietness of your own heart, you know that you've got a problem that others can ... or could ... or will see, check which source you're connected to. "Apart from me you can do nothing," Jesus said.

STRESS

Jesus said, "Come to me, all you who are weary and burdened, and I will give you rest. Take my yoke upon you and learn from me, for I am gentle and humble in heart, and you will find rest for your souls. For my yoke is easy and my burden is light."

MATTHEW 11:28–30

In the day of my trouble I will call to you, O LORD,
    for you will answer me.

PSALM 86:7

In my distress I called to the LORD;
    I called out to my God.
From his temple he heard my voice;
    my cry came to his ears.

2 SAMUEL 22:7

Cast your cares on the LORD
    and he will sustain you;
    he will never let the righteous fall.

PSALM 55:22

Be merciful to me, O LORD, for I am in distress;
    my eyes grow weak with sorrow,
    my soul and my body with grief.

PSALM 31:9

STRESS

When you pass through the waters,
    I will be with you;
and when you pass through the rivers,
    they will not sweep over you.
When you walk through the fire,
    you will not be burned;
    the flames will not set you ablaze.
For I am the LORD, your God.

ISAIAH 43:2–3

O LORD, you will keep in perfect peace
    him whose mind is steadfast,
    because he trusts in you.
Trust in the LORD forever,
    for the LORD, the LORD, is the Rock eternal.

ISAIAH 26:3–4

In my distress I called to the LORD;
    I cried to my God for help.
From his temple he heard my voice;
    my cry came before him, into his ears.

PSALM 18:6

I will listen to what God the LORD will say;
    he promises peace to his people.

PSALM 85:8

STRESS

When God gives any man wealth and possessions, and enables him to enjoy them, to accept his lot and be happy in his work—this is a gift of God. He seldom reflects on the days of his life, because God keeps him occupied with gladness of heart.

ECCLESIASTES 5:19–20

Since we have been justified through faith, we have peace with God through our Lord Jesus Christ, through whom we have gained access by faith into this grace in which we now stand. And we rejoice in the hope of the glory of God.

ROMANS 5:1–2

This is what the Sovereign LORD, the Holy One of Israel, says: "In repentance and rest is your salvation, in quietness and trust is your strength."

ISAIAH 30:15

Because so many people were coming and going that the apostles did not even have a chance to eat, Jesus said to them, "Come with me by yourselves to a quiet place and get some rest."

MARK 6:31

STRESS

"I will refresh the weary and satisfy the faint," says the LORD.

JEREMIAH 31:25

Remember the Sabbath day by keeping it holy. Six days you shall labor and do all your work, but the seventh day is a Sabbath to the LORD your God. On it you shall not do any work, neither you, nor your son or daughter. . . . For in six days the LORD made the heavens and the earth, the sea, and all that is in them, but he rested on the seventh day. Therefore the LORD blessed the Sabbath day and made it holy.

EXODUS 20:8–11

The LORD makes me lie down in green pastures,
    he leads me beside quiet waters,
    he restores my soul.
He guides me in paths of righteousness
    for his name's sake.

PSALM 23:2–3

Jesus said, "Do not let your hearts be troubled. Trust in God; trust also in me."

JOHN 14:1

Let us not become weary in doing good, for at the proper time we will reap a harvest if we do not give up.

GALATIANS 6:9

Consider it pure joy, my brothers, whenever you face trials of many kinds, because you know that the testing of your faith develops perseverance. Perseverance must finish its work so that you may be mature and complete, not lacking anything.

JAMES 1:2-4

DEVOTIONAL THOUGHT ON STRESS

Have you ever been completely frozen? I'm not talking about the kind of frozen that happens when a sub-zero wind chill cuts through your warmest winter clothing, or the kind of frozen that happens when your engine oil reservoir runs dry. I'm talking about the frozen that comes when stress and pressure bring you to the breaking point.

Sometimes the circumstances of life stop us cold. Sometimes family pressures and work stress leave us frozen in our tracks, completely unable to move. But when we have completely run out of answers, when our solutions are woefully inadequate, when our energy and our desire to go on have vanished, God's Holy Spirit picks up the phone on the first ring. "Love, joy, peace, patience, kindness, goodness, faithfulness, gentleness and self-control" (Galatians 5:33–23) are then ours for the asking.

Let the sovereign God of the universe thaw your cold heart. Let his grace free your aching soul. Be filled with his Spirit ... he'll deliver you. I promise.

Success

The LORD said, "Be strong and very courageous. Be careful to obey all the law my servant Moses gave you; do not turn from it to the right or to the left, that you may be successful wherever you go. Do not let this Book of the Law depart from your mouth; meditate on it day and night, so that you may be careful to do everything written in it. Then you will be prosperous and successful."

JOSHUA 1:7–8

King Uzziah sought God during the days of Zechariah, who instructed him in the fear of God. As long as he sought the Lord, God gave him success.

2 CHRONICLES 26:5

Blessed is the man
    who does not walk in the counsel of the wicked
or stand in the way of sinners
    or sit in the seat of mockers.
But his delight is in the law of the LORD,
    and on his law he meditates day and night.
He is like a tree planted by streams of water,
    which yields its fruit in season
and whose leaf does not wither.
    Whatever he does prospers.

PSALM 1:1–3

SUCCESS

Hezekiah trusted in the LORD, the God of Israel. There was no one like him among all the kings of Judah, either before him or after him. He held fast to the LORD and did not cease to follow him; he kept the commands the LORD had given Moses. The LORD was with him; he was successful in whatever he undertook.

2 KINGS 18:5-7

Have faith in the Lord your God and you will be upheld; have faith in his prophets and you will be successful.

2 CHRONICLES 20:20

When his master saw that the LORD was with him and that the LORD gave him success in everything he did, Joseph found favor in his eyes and became his attendant. Potiphar put him in charge of his household, and he entrusted to his care everything he owned.

GENESIS 39:3-4

In everything that King Hezekiah undertook in the service of God's temple and in obedience to the law and the commands, he sought his God and worked wholeheartedly. And so he prospered.

2 CHRONICLES 31:21

SUCCESS

———

Commit to the Lord whatever you do,
and your plans will succeed.

PROVERBS 16:3

May the LORD give you the desire of your heart
and make all your plans succeed.
We will shout for joy when you are victorious
and will lift up our banners in the
name of our God.
May the LORD grant all your requests.

PSALM 20:4–5

Plans fail for lack of counsel,
but with many advisers they succeed.

PROVERBS 15:22

DEVOTIONAL THOUGHT ON SUCCESS

Let's take a little journey back to geometry class. We're going to discuss postulates. For an example, let's try a family postulate. If I am married and if my wife gives birth to a baby, then I am a father. If I make a rule and my child disobeys me, then I have some disciplining work to do. Since the first part of each statement is true, and since the second part of each statement is also true, then the combination of the first and second parts make each conclusion true for sure. See how these work?

In Deuteronomy 30 we have an amazing postulate. It starts with verse one and ends with verse three. Moses presented this amazing postulate to the Israelites in terms they could clearly understand: Since God can be taken at his word, if he finds you obedient to his law, then he will "restore your fortunes ... and have compassion on you."

While theologians will arm-wrestle over the kind of "prosperity" God is referring to here, it's indisputable that he does promise the kind of success that is consistent within his economy—where a foreign import can be bought with lunch money and where a happy family is a priceless treasure.

THANKFULNESS

Praise the LORD.
Give thanks to the LORD, for he is good;
    his love endures forever.

PSALM 106:1

I will extol the LORD at all times;
    his praise will always be on my lips.

PSALM 34:1

By prayer and petition, with thanksgiving, present your
requests to God.

PHILIPPIANS 4:6

Give thanks in all circumstances, for this is God's will
for you in Christ Jesus.

1 THESSALONIANS 5:18

Thanks be to God! He gives us the victory through our
Lord Jesus Christ.

1 CORINTHIANS 15:57

I will give thanks to the LORD because of
    his righteousness
and will sing praise to the name of the
    LORD Most High.

PSALM 7:17

THANKFULNESS

*Just as you received Christ Jesus as Lord, continue to
live in him, rooted and built up in him, strengthened
in the faith as you were taught, and overflowing with
thankfulness.*

COLOSSIANS 2:6–7

*Thanks be to God, who always leads us in triumphal
procession in Christ and through us spreads everywhere
the fragrance of the knowledge of him.*

2 CORINTHIANS 2:14

Let them give thanks to the LORD for
    his unfailing love
and his wonderful deeds for men.

PSALM 107:21

You turned my wailing into dancing;
    you removed my sackcloth
    and clothed me with joy,
that my heart may sing to you and not be silent.
    O LORD my God, I will give you thanks forever.

PSALM 30:11–12

Enter the LORD's gates with thanksgiving
    and his courts with praise;
    give thanks to him and praise his name.

PSALM 100:4

THANKFULNESS

———

Come, let us sing for joy to the LORD;
>   let us shout aloud to the Rock of our salvation.
Let us come before him with thanksgiving
>   and extol him with music and song.

PSALM 95:1–2

Thanks be to God for his indescribable gift!

2 CORINTHIANS 9:15

I will extol the LORD with all my heart
>   in the council of the upright
>   and in the assembly.
Great are the works of the LORD;
>   they are pondered by all who delight in them.

PSALM 111:1–2

Let the peace of Christ rule in your hearts, since as members of one body you were called to peace. And be thankful. Let the word of Christ dwell in you richly as you teach and admonish one another with all wisdom, and as you sing psalms, hymns and spiritual songs with gratitude in your hearts to God. And whatever you do, whether in word or deed, do it all in the name of the Lord Jesus, giving thanks to God the Father through him.

COLOSSIANS 3:15–17

DEVOTIONAL THOUGHT ON
THANKFULNESS

There has always been something very unusual about Billy Webb. It took me a while to figure out what was so special about this particular friend.

Then one day it hit me. Billy is a handwritten-thank-you-note man. From the very first time we met for lunch until our most recent outing, I've received a note in the mail a few days later from him. These notes are not long and drawn out; in fact, they usually fit on one side of a four-by-six card. But even when he has picked up the tab for lunch, Billy thanks me for my time and for my friendship.

The apostle Paul opened nearly every one of his thirteen New Testament letters with a "thank you." The letter to the church in Philippi is especially strong. "I thank my God every time I remember you. In all my prayers for all of you, I always pray with joy because of your partnership in the gospel," he wrote (Philippians 1:3–5).

Are you a thank-you-note man in the lives of your children, family, and friends? Being such a man only takes a moment, but the dividends are astonishing. Try it. You'll see.

TRUST

Those who know your name will trust in you,
> for you, LORD, have never forsaken
> those who seek you.

PSALM 9:10

Those who trust in the LORD are like Mount Zion,
> which cannot be shaken but endures forever.

PSALM 125:1

It is better to take refuge in the LORD
> than to trust in man.
It is better to take refuge in the LORD
> than to trust in princes.

PSALM 118:8–9

Why are you downcast, O my soul?
> Why so disturbed within me?
Put your hope in God,
> for I will yet praise him,
> my Savior and my God.

PSALM 42:5–6

Blessed is he whose help is the God of Jacob,
> whose hope is in the LORD his God.

PSALM 146:5

TRUST

Whoever gives heed to instruction prospers,
and blessed is he who trusts in the LORD.

PROVERBS 16:20

Blessed is the man who trusts in the LORD,
whose confidence is in him.
He will be like a tree planted by the water
that sends out its roots by the stream.
It does not fear when heat comes;
its leaves are always green.
It has no worries in a year of drought
and never fails to bear fruit.

JEREMIAH 17:7-8

Trust in the LORD and do good;
dwell in the land and enjoy safe pasture.

PSALM 37:3

*Nebuchadnezzar said, "Praise be to the God of
Shadrach, Meshach and Abednego, who has sent his
angel and rescued his servants! They trusted in him and
defied the king's command and were willing to give up
their lives rather than serve or worship any god except
their own God."*

DANIEL 3:28

TRUST

He who trusts in the LORD will prosper.

PROVERBS 28:25

Anyone who trusts in Jesus will never be put to shame.

ROMANS 10:11

Fear of man will prove to be a snare,
    but whoever trusts in the LORD is kept safe.

PROVERBS 29:25

Trust in the LORD with all your heart
    and lean not on your own understanding.

PROVERBS 3:5

Be strong and take heart,
    all you who hope in the LORD.

PSALM 31:24

The LORD is good,
    a refuge in times of trouble.
He cares for those who trust in him.

NAHUM 1:7

Devotional Thought on Trust

Our family had flown to southern California. At exactly 3:30 the next morning, I woke to something I had never heard before. It was a cracking sound, reminiscent of lifting a sticking window sash. And then, incredibly, our hotel room began to roll. Earthquake! When we saw the news the next morning, we saw freeways—the very ones we had traveled only hours before—twisted and broken.

As I watched the local news shows and listened to the trembling voices of the victims, I learned that the lack of warning and property damage are not the worst parts of living through these natural disasters. No, the greatest ruin an earthquake delivers is in the hearts of people who can no longer count on the dependability of solid ground. Terra firma has lost its firma.

What can you count on ... your job, your car, your Maytag? How about your stock portfolio? Your relationships? Your health?

None of these things are worthy of our absolute trust. Incredible as it may sound, they will all let us down. But trusting in God will never bring disappointment. He is enough. His reliability is legendary. His faithfulness is completely sure ... absolutely firma.

VALUES

One man gives freely, yet gains even more;
    another withholds unduly,
      but comes to poverty.

PROVERBS 11:24

*Jesus said, "If you do good to those who are good to
you, what credit is that to you? Even 'sinners' do that.
And if you lend to those from whom you expect repay-
ment, what credit is that to you? Even 'sinners' lend to
'sinners,' expecting to be repaid in full. But love your
enemies, do good to them, and lend to them without
expecting to get anything back. Then your reward will
be great, and you will be sons of the Most High. . . .
Be merciful, just as your Father is merciful."*

LUKE 6:33–36

Who may ascend the hill of the LORD?
    Who may stand in his holy place?
He who has clean hands and a pure heart,
    who does not lift up his soul to an idol
      for swear by what is false.
He will receive blessing from the LORD
    and vindication from God his Savior.

PSALM 24:3–5

VALUES

What does the LORD require of you?
To act justly and to love mercy
and to walk humbly with your God.

MICAH 6:8

Give me only my daily bread, O LORD.
Otherwise, I may have too much and disown you
and say, "Who is the LORD?"
Or I may become poor and steal,
and so dishonor the name of my God.

PROVERBS 30:8–9

*Jesus said, "'Love the Lord your God with all your heart
and with all your soul and with all your mind.' This is
the first and greatest commandment. And the second is
like it: 'Love your neighbor as yourself.'"*

MATTHEW 22:37–39

*Speak and act as those who are going to be judged by
the law that gives freedom, because judgment without
mercy will be shown to anyone who has not been merciful. Mercy triumphs over judgment!*

JAMES 2:12–13

Be careful that you do not forget the LORD your God, failing to observe his commands, his laws and his decrees. ... Otherwise, when you eat and are satisfied, when you build fine houses and settle down, and when your herds and flocks grow large and your silver and gold increase and all you have is multiplied, then your heart will become proud and you will forget the LORD your God.

DEUTERONOMY 8:11–14

Do to others as you would have them do to you.

LUKE 6:31

Jesus said, "When you give a banquet, invite the poor, the crippled, the lame, the blind, and you will be blessed. Although they cannot repay you, you will be repaid at the resurrection of the righteous."

LUKE 14:13–14

DEVOTIONAL THOUGHT ON VALUES

Some guidelines are absolute. The Ten Commandments, for example, never change. It is never right to commit adultery, murder someone, or love anything more than you love God. But other things are more like keys on a piano. The notes are not right or wrong by themselves; it depends on how they're played within a song.

For example, fighting seems like a bad thing. But throughout the Bible God allows fighting to protect one's family or one's country. Compassion is considered a good thing, yet at times we must put our feelings aside to see that justice is not ignored.

With God's wisdom and good counsel from godly people, we can learn to do the right thing when the line between right and wrong is not clear. Solomon said, "Wisdom is supreme; therefore get wisdom. Though it cost all you have, get understanding" (Proverbs 4:7). This only comes from God.

WISDOM

If you call out for insight
  and cry aloud for understanding,
and if you look for it as for silver
  and search for it as for hidden treasure,
then you will understand the fear of the LORD
  and find the knowledge of God.
For the LORD gives wisdom,
  and from his mouth come
  knowledge and understanding.

PROVERBS 2:3-6

The fear of the LORD—that is wisdom,
and to shun evil is understanding.

JOB 28:28

*Jesus said, "Everyone who hears these words of mine
and puts them into practice is like a wise man who
built his house on the rock. The rain came down, the
streams rose, and the winds blew and beat against that
house; yet it did not fall, because it had its foundation
on the rock."*

MATTHEW 7:24-25

Get wisdom, get understanding. ...
Do not forsake wisdom, and she will protect you;
  love her, and she will watch over you.

WISDOM

Wisdom is supreme; therefore get wisdom.
>Though it cost all you have, get understanding.

PROVERBS 4:5-7

Trust in the LORD with all your heart
>and lean not on your own understanding;
in all your ways acknowledge him,
>and he will make your paths straight.

PROVERBS 3:5-6

Do you not know?
>Have you not heard?
The LORD is the everlasting God,
>the Creator of the ends of the earth.
He will not grow tired or weary,
>and his understanding no one can fathom.
He gives strength to the weary
>and increases the power of the weak.

ISAIAH 40:28-29

Whether you turn to the right or to the left, your ears will hear a voice behind you, saying, "This is the way; walk in it."

ISAIAH 30:21

WISDOM

The wisdom that comes from heaven is first of all pure; then peace-loving, considerate, submissive, full of mercy and good fruit, impartial and sincere.

JAMES 3:17

Where then does wisdom come from?
Where does understanding dwell?
It is hidden from the eyes of every living thing,
concealed even from the birds of the air. . . .
God understands the way to it
and he alone knows where it dwells.

JOB 28:20–21, 23

The foolishness of God is wiser than man's wisdom, and the weakness of God is stronger than man's strength.

1 CORINTHIANS 1:25

Wisdom calls,
"Whoever listens to me will live in safety
and be at ease, without fear of harm."

PROVERBS 1:33

If any of you lacks wisdom, he should ask God, who gives generously to all without finding fault, and it will be given to him.

JAMES 1:5

DEVOTIONAL THOUGHT ON
WISDOM

———

Solomon will forever be remembered as Israel's wisest king. And, no doubt, he would have bragged about how bright his children were as well. But wise old Solomon didn't leave anything to chance; he didn't just figure that his children would pick up this wisdom on their own.

The book of Proverbs is actually a love note to Solomon's children. Wise and wealthy as he was, Solomon stopped and took the time to pour this wisdom into his children. As a result of his efforts, men and women throughout history have basked in the glow of these wise words.

Do you wonder where Solomon got the idea to give this wisdom to his children himself? How did he figure out that they probably wouldn't just pick it up on their own?

David told his son just before his own death, "Be strong, show yourself a man, and observe what the LORD your God requires" (1 Kings 2:2–3). What a good idea, Solomon must have thought to himself as he shuffled off to his bedroom. When I have children of my own, I think I'll do the same.

Like father, like son.

WORK

When God gives any man wealth and possessions, and enables him to enjoy them, to accept his lot and be happy in his work—this is a gift of God.

ECCLESIASTES 5:19

Always give yourselves fully to the work of the Lord, because you know that your labor in the Lord is not in vain.

1 CORINTHIANS 15:58

Whatever your hand finds to do, do it with all your might.

ECCLESIASTES 9:10

Jesus said, "I know your deeds, your hard work and your perseverance. . . . You have persevered and have endured hardships for my name, and have not grown weary."

REVELATION 2:2–3

Whatever you do, work at it with all your heart, as working for the Lord, not for men, since you know that you will receive an inheritance from the Lord as a reward.

COLOSSIANS 3:23–24

Work

All hard work brings a profit.

PROVERBS 14:23

May the favor of the Lord our God rest upon us;
establish the work of our hands for us.

PSALM 90:17

*Be strong and do not give up, for your work will be
rewarded.*

2 CHRONICLES 15:7

*The LORD will open the heavens, the storehouse of his
bounty, to send rain on your land in season and to bless
all the work of your hands.*

DEUTERONOMY 28:12

*For six days, work is to be done, but the seventh day
shall be your holy day, a Sabbath of rest to the LORD.*

EXODUS 35:2

The desires of the diligent are fully satisfied.

PROVERBS 13:4

The plans of the diligent lead to profit
as surely as haste leads to poverty.

PROVERBS 21:5

WORK

———

Sow your seed in the morning,
and at evening let not your hands be idle,
for you do not know which will succeed,
whether this or that,
or whether both will do equally well.

ECCLESIASTES 11:6

Make it your ambition to lead a quiet life, to mind your own business and to work with your hands, ... so that your daily life may win the respect of outsiders and so that you will not be dependent on anybody.

1 THESSALONIANS 4:11–12

Jesus said, "Well done, good and faithful servant! You have been faithful with a few things; I will put you in charge of many things. Come and share your master's happiness!"

MATTHEW 25:21

DEVOTIONAL THOUGHT ON WORK

King Solomon provides us with an employment choice. "You can trade the sweat and toil behind door number two for the box that Johnny is bringing down the aisle right now."

"I'll take the box," we say without thinking. "Purposeless work is not for me."

As Solomon lifts the top off the box, we hear these words: "Everyone may eat and drink, and find satisfaction in all his toil—this is a gift from God" (Ecclesiastes 3:13). Did you hear that? Work is a not a curse. Work is a blessing.

You spend more of your waking hours engaged in work than in any other activity. Can you imagine that your gracious heavenly Father, the one who has given you life and who lovingly sustains it, would want you to dread the largest slice of your life? Not a chance.

Carefully examine what you're doing with your work. Is the work of your hands satisfying to you? Do you feel God's blessing on your labor? If the answer is yes to these questions, you've got something to be thankful for. If it's no, this may be a good time to take a careful look at what you're doing.

A WORD ABOUT THE AUTHOR

Robert Wolgemuth has been in the publishing business for 25 years. He is the owner and president of Wolgemuth & Associates, Inc., a literary agency exclusively representing the writing work of approximately twenty authors including Joni Eareckson Tada, Ravi Zacharias, R.C. Sproul, Orel Hershiser, Patrick Morley, and Henry Blackaby.

Robert is a speaker and best-selling author. His books include, *She Calls Me Daddy*, *The Devotional Bible for Dads*, *Daddy@Work*, and *What's in the Bible: The Story of God through Time and Eternity*, a co-written work between Wolgemuth and Dr. R.C. Sproul. His other collaborative works include *O Worship the King* with Joni Eareckson Tada and Dr. John MacArthur, and *Between the Lines: Nine Principles to Live By* with Orel Hershiser.

A speaking and consulting resource for groups including DreamWorks, the Professional Golfers Association, Taylor University, Vanderbilt University Children's Hospital, The Maryland Science Center, Belmont University, Focus on the Family, Willow Creek Community Church, and The Foundation, Robert is known as a champion for the family, effective communication, leadership, listening skills, relationship building, and traditional values.

Among his professional accomplishments, he was selected as an Outstanding Young Man in America in 1978, Who's Who in America in 1980, Who's Who in Business and Industry in 1982, and served two terms as the Chairman of the Evangelical Christian Publishers Association.

A 1969 graduate of Taylor University, Mr. Wolgemuth is the father of two grown daughters, two sons-in-law, and three grandchildren. He and Bobbie, his wife of over 31 years, live in Central Florida.

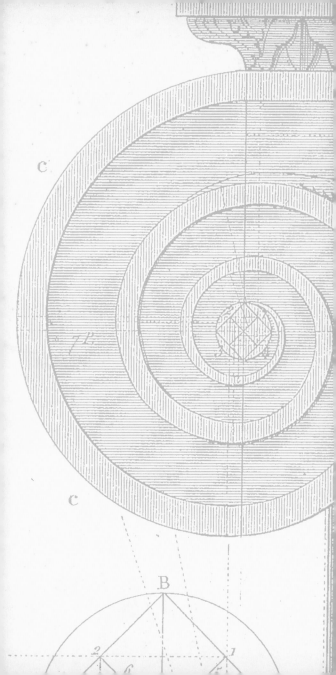